The Obedience of Faith

THE OBEDIENCE OF FAITH

The Story of
Rev. Christine A. Gibson
Founder of
ZION BIBLE INSTITUTE

by
Rev. Mary Campbell Wilson

VICTORY HOUSE, INC.
TULSA, OK

All Scriptures are taken from the King James Version of the Holy Bible, except as noted. Some passages have been paraphrased by the author, based on the King James Version.

Copyright © 1993 by Zion Bible Institute, Inc.

All rights reserved. This book is protected under the copyright laws of the United States of America. No part of this book, including the cover, may be copied or reprinted without permission from the publisher.

Printed in the United States of America.

ISBN: 0-932081-32-0

Published by Zion Bible Institute
27 Middle Highway
Barrington, Rhode Island 02806, and
Victory House, Inc.
P.O. Box 700238
Tulsa, Oklahoma 74170

Edited by: Patricia P. Pickard with Lloyd B. Hildebrand

Cover design by: Cosmic Cowboy Design

Acknowledgments

For the final preparation of this book, I owe a debt of gratitude and love to Patricia and Carroll Pickard of Bangor, Maine, who invited me to their seasonal home in Florida in the winter of 1992 after the death of my precious mother. It has long been my desire to write a book about the life and work of Rev. Christine A. Gibson. Unforeseeable circumstances had prevented my finishing it until I went to Florida.

There, in the peaceful atmosphere of their home, I was able to gather my thoughts and materials together. Pat, with her knowledge of computers, love for words, and understanding of my desire to finish what I had started several years ago, came to my rescue. She put many hours of work into the story, and as we worked together, the blessing of the Lord came upon us many times. Without her, I could not have completed *The Obedience of Faith*.

Paul, in writing to the Romans concerning Phoebe, a sister of the Church, recorded these words, "She hath been a helper of many, and of myself also." Pat has been my Phoebe, and we will always remember our labors of love over this book.

M.C.W.
August 15, 1992

Contents

Foreword by Dr. Benjamin Crandall............................vii
Preface ix
Introduction..xi

Chapter 1
    Zion, the Joy of the Whole Earth 1
Chapter 2
    Early Days of Conversion.................................... 7
Chapter 3
    Not Knowing Whither She Went 15
Chapter 4
    Deliverance From a Snare...................................19
Chapter 5
    I Being in the Way, the Lord Led Me 25
Chapter 6
    Not You...But God..31
Chapter 7
    Visions and Revelations.....................................37
Chapter 8
    Your Life Is Hidden With Christ in God 41
Chapter 9
    With God Nothing Shall Be Impossible 45
Chapter 10
    This Is That Spoken by the Prophet Joel................51
Chapter 11
    When I Am Weak, Then Am I Strong 59

Chapter 12
  Have the Faith of God 69
Chapter 13
  Though It Tarry, Wait for It 79
Chapter 14
  The Exercise of Faith 87
Chapter 15
  Holding Fast the Confidence 103
Chapter 16
  Great Is Thy Faithfulness 113
Chapter 17
  The Bugle Call Is Given 127
Chapter 18
  Enlarge the Place of Thy Tent...........................137
Chapter 19
  The Operation of Faith 141
Chapter 20
  Through Faith They Obtained...........................153
Chapter 21
  The Alpha and Omega.....................................157
Appendix A — Sermon: "Saviors or Judges?" —
                Rev. C. A. Gibson 165
          B — Sermon: "Signs of the Times" —
                Rev. R. A. Gibson 173
          C — Faith Home Reports, 1913-1915 183
          D — Chronology....................................191
Photographs
About the Author by Patricia P. Pickard

Foreword

Paul, in his second letter to Timothy, reminds us of the influence godly women have in the shaping of lives and the building of faith. He wrote, "When I call to remembrance the unfeigned faith that is in thee, which dwelt first in thy grandmother Lois, and thy mother Eunice; and I am persuaded that in thee also" (2 Tim. 1:5).

No woman (or man, for that matter), other than my own mother, had a greater influence on my life than Christine Gibson. She was my "Lois," a woman with unfeigned faith, tremendous courage, and rich, spiritual insights. From her, I learned (through her personal example) that our number-one priority should always be to stand with God — His will and His ways — no matter how unpopular that stand might be.

Sister Gibson was an inspiring teacher — a chosen vessel unto whom God imparted many spiritual gifts and graces. She had the rare capacity to show the truth through vivid images, analogies and metaphors that God had given to her. Most importantly, however, she showed the truth by the way she lived.

My mentor, Sister Christine Gibson, knew the truth described in Galatians 5:6b — "The only thing that counts is faith expressing itself through love" (NIV). Her unshakeable faith compelled her to obey our Lord's supreme commandment: "And Jesus answered him, The first of all the commandments is, Hear, O Israel; The Lord our God is one Lord: And thou shalt love the Lord thy God with all thy heart, and with all thy soul, and with all thy mind, and with all thy strength: this is the first commandment. And the second is like [it], namely this,

Thou shalt love thy neighbour as thyself. There is none other commandment greater than these" (Mark 12:29-31).

To all Zionians, Sister Gibson was a true mother in Zion. She taught, nurtured and cared for us as if we were her own children. She prayed for us, encouraged and inspired us, and because of her love and concern, we were able to hold onto the truth that, "Though the road may be long, our Savior is strong, and He holds our hand."

The vision God gave to Sister Gibson — one of Zion becoming the joy of the whole earth — is being fulfilled in our present day because this extraordinary lady, a handmaiden of the Lord, was faithful unto death. It was her *Obedience of Faith* that has enabled each Zionian to know more fully the eternal plan and purpose of God, namely: "And the ransomed of the Lord shall return, and come to Zion with songs and everlasting joy upon their heads: they shall obtain joy and gladness, and sorrow and sighing shall flee away" (Isa. 35:10).

Dr. Benjamin Crandall, President
Zion Bible Institute
Barrington, Rhode Island

Preface

The year was 1986. Friends were urging me to write about my friend and pastor, Rev. Christine A. Gibson. As I prayed about this, I realized the importance of recording the details of her life of faith as I had heard them from her own lips, read them from her own writings, and witnessed them first-hand.

So many details — and so little time. My first manuscript had been worked on, many times hurriedly, without adequate time to search out all the details I needed. Kind friends had typed the original manuscript for me and it had lain quietly in dark resting places for many months and years due to many circumstances that had taken place. However, I feel that now is the time for me to set forth this exciting story as it should be told. It is an account that is worthy of note.

This book shares the story of a life of faith, a life of hope, a life of charity, and a life of vision. Christine Gibson was a heroine of faith, an inspiration to all who knew her, a gentle lady, a friend to all. She was filled with perseverance, love, and trust in God. She had hands willing to work, a heart willing to serve, and feet willing to go. She gave her all so that thousands of young men and women could go forth into the harvest field and work for the cause of Christ.

Many years ago, when Sister Gibson was requested to write the story of her life, she chose to write under the title, *The Obedience of Faith*. I feel that this is a most appropriate title for this woman to choose. For this reason, I have selected the same title for the present volume.

Due to her last illness, Sister Gibson was not able to complete her memoirs. Thus, her story was never finished, nor was it ever published. Along with portions of her own writings, I include the songs and poems she recorded in her original manuscript.

"By faith Abraham, when he was called to go out into a place which he should after receive for an inheritance, obeyed; and he went out, not knowing whither he went" (Heb. 11:8).

During 1905, like Abraham of old, and through unusual workings of God, Christine Eckman was called to leave her country and kindred and start out on a voyage which was to afterwards bring her to the place God had planned for her inheritance.

It was a joy to discover, as we worked on this book, that the cornerstone of the magnificent Peck Estate in Barrington, Rhode Island, which is now the home of Zion Bible Institute, is dated 1905, the exact year when Christine came to America. "O the depth of the riches both of the wisdom and knowledge of God! How unsearchable are his judgments and his ways past finding out! For who hath known the mind of the Lord? (Rom. 11:33,34a).

I salute this Mother in Israel, and dedicate this feeble effort to celebrate her life of total abandonment to God. My prayer is that those who read this book will follow in her footsteps. A true handmaiden of the Lord — Christine Amelia Eckman Gibson.

Mary Campbell Wilson

Bangor, Maine
1992

Introduction

In order to have a better understanding and a deeper realization of the providential leadings of God upon Zion Bible Institute, Zion Gospel Temple, and in the life of the founder of the school, the Rev. Christine A. Gibson, a brief history of the Temple, and also of Faith Home, is herein presented.

The first regular services of the church, which is now called Zion Gospel Temple, began on January 1, 1877, with the Rev. Alpheus Angel Cleveland and his wife, Adelaide Marian Cleveland, as pastors. The name of the church was simply "Faith Church" (and many times referred to as the Mission Church) until 1900 when it was formally organized as "The Church of the First Born."

Rev. and Mrs. Alpheus Angel Cleveland were married on March 28, 1865, less than a month before the end of the Civil War in America.

In 1900, Rev. Cleveland authored a book, *The Remembered Way*, which gives insight into his ministry:

> I was converted in 1855, and sanctified by the Holy Spirit in 1857. I then heard the Voice, *"Go work today in my vineyard."* I answered, "Yes," not knowing it meant to preach the word in season and out of season. But God, whose own good hour most surely comes, led me to take a four-year educational course, beginning at the Conference Seminary in East Greenwich, Rhode Island. I continued afterward, in that ever-remembered School of the Prophets, The

Theological Seminary at Concord, New Hampshire. I was married to Miss Addie M. Dickinson, March 22, 1865, while I was a student at East Greenwich. But *her* education had already been accomplished in the home of suffering — a preparation for her most earnest life among the people.

God impressed our minds with the thought of a *HOME* for his troubled and bewildered ones. The passage in 2 Samuel 7:10, was given unto me: "Moreover, I will appoint a place for my people Israel, and will plant them, that they may dwell in a place of their own, and move no more; neither shall the children of wickedness afflict them any more, as beforetime." It would be vain to attempt to describe the sweetness with which the Spirit sealed this Scripture. It was another link in the chain of divine purpose concerning me. He further unfolded to me that it was in His plan to take me out of the work in which I was engaged, and transfer me to another. This proved to be the *FAITH WORK*. Nothing could meet the divine requirement, but to step forth, entirely free from every human dependence, and lean only on the Everlasting Arm.

From the hour that the Lord called me to forsake my home, my friends, my native town [Barre, Vermont], and go out into His vineyard, for fifteen years [1861-1876], it was His purpose for us to move eighteen times. Welcome, indeed, was the promise given in the Spirit, *"I will appoint you a Home of your own, and you shall move no more."*

Sister Addie made entries in a diary which continue the story:

November 30, 1876, Thanksgiving. As we came out of church, a brother from Watchemoket — a village two miles from East Providence center — asked us to come down on the Sabbath, and preach for a new society. The baptism of God is so resting upon us, that work is a necessity.

January 1, 1877. Perpetual summer with its freshness and greenness, and the singing of birds, reigns in my soul. Uninterrupted union and communion with God prevails. Nothing disturbs the serenity of my soul. We have entered upon our new work at Watchemoket — an abundant opportunity for all spiritual and physical energies.

February 24, 1877. A large house is empty, and Mr. Cleveland was told, upon inquiry, we were welcome to occupy it. This is of God. The owner's wife sent us blankets and bedding. Now we have this most beautiful home, favorable for rest and study. The thought comes sometimes, that the Lord intends this house for a *FAITH HOME*.

March 20, 1877. We were greatly surprised by a visit of twenty-one *donation* brethren and sisters. We proposed a spiritual season; and the Holy Ghost came down in power. For two hours, the meeting went on with unabated zeal.

March 31, 1877. Mr. Cleveland is convinced that he is to disconnect himself from Conference at its approaching session. It is my conviction that we are to set ourselves apart for a *FAITH WORK*.

April 25, 1877. We started for Boston and Dover [New Hampshire]. Mr. Cleveland withdrew from Conference. We came to East Rochester [New

Hampshire]. Old friends crowd about us, and on Tuesday evening, we had a meeting — a precious season.

May 21, 1877. Mr. Cleveland has opened a hall for worship. He preached in the morning, and I spoke in the evening.

June 10, 1877. Mr. Cleveland announced after his sermon today, that this is a *FAITH WORK*. He read the report of the past four weeks: $21.90 for provisions, organ, and pulpit. In the evening, I spoke at the hall and the school house, and the Lord gave me great liberty.

June 28, 1877. God has now brought us where He can accomplish His purpose concerning us. I have a glorious assurance that prayer has prevailed.

Sister Addie Cleveland died on March 26, 1879, at forty-two years of age. Brother Cleveland's writings pick up the story:

The conviction grew upon me that God wanted a *HOME* for His little ones who were without a resting place. The conviction intensified as months multiplied into years. One day, after fourteen years had passed [1876-1890], I remarked, "How is my soul straightened until it be accomplished." A few days later, I heard of a vacated house, most conveniently located, and I said, "It is the place, that, for fourteen years I have been praying for. I want it."

On December 15, 1890, we [By 1882, Rev. Cleveland had remarried.] took possession, in the name of the Lord, and *THE FAITH HOME* was opened. Without advertising, the rooms were soon taken. We are now in the tenth year of its history

[1890-1900], and we can affirm that all needs have been supplied.

This home, located at 846 Broadway, had been built in the 1870s by Captain George B. Hull, a seaman. He had sold it to another gentleman who later defaulted on the payments. Thus, the property reverted back to Captain Hull.

One day when Rev. Cleveland was riding past this home in his horse and buggy, he felt an inward urge to stop. He jumped from the buggy and rang the doorbell. When Captain Hull came to the door, Mr. Cleveland asked him if the house was for sale. "No," replied the retired sea captain, "I just reacquired this, having recently retired from many years of seafaring." Mr. Cleveland thanked him and went on his way.

Several days passed, and once more, as Mr. Cleveland was riding near the house, he felt led to stop and ask the same question. This time Captain Hull emphatically told him that the house was not for sale. Mr. Cleveland thanked him and went on his way for the second time.

However, a few weeks later, as Mr. Cleveland was again driving on Broadway, he noticed that a "For Sale" sign had been placed in front of the house. Mr. Cleveland was quite amazed and excitedly jumped from his buggy, rang the bell, and soon was in negotiations with Captain Hull. Mr. Cleveland purchased this home and continued his work for God at that location, ministering mostly to aged missionaries.

He continued to pastor the flock at the little rented hall, and after being there for several years, the congregation moved to the parlors of Faith Home where they conducted services for four years following. The congregation grew, and they started looking for larger quarters.

A new building, called the Leslie Block, was erected at 150 Taunton Avenue, East Providence, and Faith Church moved into a hall on the second floor of that structure. This congregation was formally organized on June 19, 1900 under the name, "The Church of the First Born."

Rev. Cleveland died on August 10, 1908, just a few months after turning the work over to Christine Eckman. On November 10, 1910, Christine married the Rev. Reuben A. Gibson and they pastored the work together for a period of time. On November 30, 1910, the church was incorporated.

Property was subsequently purchased on the west side of Ivy Street near Taunton Avenue. A church building was erected there, with the first service being held on February 26, 1911.

The Ivy Street property was later sold and the church moved to a newly erected chapel, located at 46 Leonard Avenue on the grounds of Faith Home. The opening service there was held on November 25, 1917.

Following the establishment of Mount Zion Bible School in 1924, and the erection of the Zion Tabernacle building, located at the corner of Leonard Avenue and Gurney Street, the church moved to the second floor of this edifice.

Rev. Reuben Gibson passed away at the time the building was being completed. Rev. Christine A. Gibson continued as pastor of the church and principal of the Bible school.

It was not until February of 1948 that the name of the church was changed from The Church of the First Born to Zion Gospel Tabernacle. Later, a new masonry building was erected at 50 Gurney Street to house this congregation. It was dedicated to God in March of 1952, and has now celebrated forty years at this location.

In November of 1954, the name of the church was changed once again, this time to Zion Gospel Temple. The following year, the church lost its pastor when the Rev. Christine A.

Gibson passed away, after forty-seven years of dedicated ministry there. Following her as pastor was the Rev. Dr. Leonard W. Heroo who had been Mrs. Gibson's associate for many years. He pastored and served the church from 1955 until 1983.

It was in the late 1950s that Faith Home no longer operated as such, and the building was then used for school purposes, thus ending the era of Faith Home at that location.

In November of 1983, the Rev. William K. Wilson was elected pastor and served until November of 1985 when the Rev. Dr. Benjamin Crandall of International Christian Center in Staten Island, New York, was officially installed as pastor of Zion Gospel Temple. Both he and his wife, the former Jeanne Bither of Houlton, Maine, are graduates of Zion Bible Institute, class of 1945.

On October 4, 1985, Zion purchased the former Barrington College in Barrington, Rhode Island, and the church services were moved to that location for a period before returning to the former location in East Providence.

In the fall of 1991, the Rev. Douglas Crandall became the new pastor of Zion Gospel Temple and remains there as of this writing.

After reading this concise introduction, you will more readily see, as you read the following chapters, how God led — step by step by step.

Chapter 1
Zion, the Joy of the Whole Earth

"**Beautiful for situation, the joy of the whole earth, is Mount Zion...**"

(Ps. 48:2).

This story begins a long time ago, on February 24, 1877, to be exact. This was the date of the establishment of a ministry in East Providence, Rhode Island, that was to be known as *FAITH HOME,* located at 846 Broadway for nearly seventy years.

Less than two years later, on January 3, 1879, in Georgetown, British Guiana, a little baby was born who would play an important role in Faith Home. No doubt thousands and thousands of little girls were born on that date, but God had a special, providential purpose in the life of this child.

The family name was Eckman and they christened their little girl Christine Amelia. Christine knew very little about her parents — only what she had been told. Her father was a Swedish captain who sailed frequently from Sweden to South America. It was on one of these trips that he met the South American lady who was to become the mother of Christine and her sister, Alice.

The loving parents died when Christine was but a little girl, and she and her sister, Alice, were brought to their grandmother's home where she cared for them. Alice was taken by relatives, and Christine was educated by one of her mother's friends, a Scottish lady who conducted a private school. This truly seemed to be the intervening providence of God, for it diverted Christine from Roman Catholicism and from entering a convent. She attended a Presbyterian church with her teacher; however, she did not know Jesus as her personal Savior at that time.

Christine received her education in this private school and her teacher found her to be an exceptionally brilliant girl. One day the headmistress of the school visited the grandmother and asked if she would consider having Christine sent to Scotland for further education. Even though the teacher sensed Christine's unusual abilities, the grandmother couldn't see sending her so far away from home. Besides this, Christine did not seem inclined or eager to leave.

Until she was about twenty years of age, Christine's life moved along as life did for most young ladies of the time. At twenty, she found herself being thrust into a worldly atmosphere to earn a living. Dancing halls and worldly amusements meant more to her than the Church. But, at the age of twenty-one, in the midst of a life of gaiety, Christine was converted.

She was employed by the government of her country in the telephone and telegraph offices and was very popular among her peers. However, they began to notice a change in her life. This change, as we shall see, was brought about as a result of several very special experiences.

One day, after working hours, one of her friends remarked that she was going to stop by a hospital to visit a Salvation Army officer who was very ill. She asked Christine to accompany her. Since it was on her way home, Christine agreed to go. After being introduced to this gentleman, a conversation followed. However, Christine seemed to be restless and in a hurry to depart, and he asked her, "What is your hurry? Where are you going?"

Christine replied, "I am attending a ball this evening and wish to get home to make preparations."

"Oh," he replied, "you are going to a ball." He then said something more which could have been considered rather crude: "A little dance, a little hell; a little dance, a little hell."

In response to this, Christine gathered up her skirts, threw her head back, and left the hospital room, later telling her friend, "Never again ask me to visit that rude, rude man!"

Christine attended the ball that evening, and as she danced through the night hours, she kept hearing the voice of the Salvation Army officer saying, "A little dance, a little hell; a little dance, a little hell."

Several days later, returning home from work, she came to a very large and lovely Catholic church that was at the corner of her street. Something within her compelled Christine to enter the church. Her steps took her directly to the altar where people were praying.

Christine knelt, closed her eyes, and began to pray in the best way that she knew. During this time of prayer, Christine received a vision from God of the bleeding Christ on Calvary's cross. Her eyes were closed, and she knew she was not looking at the statues in the sanctuary. This was a true, God-given vision of the dying Christ. She then heard the words, *Do you see that Man on the cross? He took the sinner's place. He became sin for a lost world. You are a sinner. He died in your stead. You can have His righteousness, for He is your salvation.*

The revelation came to her that through Christ's death and His shed blood, she could become a different person and live a more useful life. When Christine rose from her knees, she was definitely converted. She could have danced out of the cathedral. She was truly saved. Her sins were forgiven and she knew then and there that she was a child of God.

Christine hurried home to the apartment that she and her sister shared with another girl and told Alice what she had experienced in the church. Alice knew that her sister was very much taken up with the world of dramatics and asked, "What is this — a new play that you're interested in?"

"No," replied Christine, "it's an experience, and I would like to visit the Salvation Army barracks this evening for a meeting. Would you accompany me?"

Alice agreed to go and at the closing of the sermon, the Salvation Army officer opened the mourners' bench for people to come forward and publicly accept Jesus Christ as their Savior. Christine immediately rose to move forward when Alice grabbed her cloak and said, "You can't go down there! Don't you see who is down there? It's Bertha!" Bertha was a well-known character who lived locally; however, this did not phase Christine.

She replied, "I don't care who is down there. I only know that I need this experience and that I want it!"

Christine continued on her way to the mourners' bench and bowed in prayer. As she was praying, and others were praying for her, she felt someone move in close to her, and upon opening her eyes, Christine saw Alice receiving this beautiful experience of conversion also. This was a memorable night for the girls — the night when both Christine and Alice made their public confession that they had received Jesus Christ as their Savior.

It is interesting and significant to see the various faiths and churches which were involved in Christine's conversion. It was an indication of the life she would live. She would be touching many, many people from many walks of life.

Some months later, Christine and Alice united with a Holiness group at a Full Gospel Mission in Georgetown, and they were baptized in water.

It was at this time in Christine's life that she met the Rev. Reuben Gibson who preached occasionally at the mission. This man of God was greatly esteemed by Alice and Christine for his godly life and helpfulness to the young people of the mission. Prior to their acquaintance, Rev. Gibson had met with a great misfortune in his domestic affairs, and later left the area and went to America, taking his five young children with him.

The girls at Christine's place of employment marveled at the change in her and expressed an opinion that it would not last. However, they did request an invitation to attend Christine's water baptism service that was going to be conducted by her pastor, Rev. Penney. She invited them, and as she was going down into the waters of baptism, she saw the girls laughing and nudging each other. As she came up out of the water, it seems that she heard the words, *A great gulf is fixed.* And truly, it was fixed. Christine's life was never the same again.

Chapter 2
Early Days of Conversion

"Therefore, if any man be in Christ, he is a new creature; old things are passed away, behold, all things are become new"

(2 Cor. 5:17).

Does conversion make a difference? Yes, it clearly does. If there is no difference, there is no conversion.

Christine Eckman was a high-spirited, worldly, and quick-tempered young woman. However, as God worked in her life, many of these infirmities and weaknesses left.

The custom in the office where Christine worked was to make a hot drink just before the office crew left at the end of their day's work. They would drink hot chocolate, talk over the happenings of the day, and each would go on his/her way. Each week one of the girls took a turn making the hot drink. One day a rather clumsy girl made the cocoa. Christine happened to be walking past her at this time, on her way to a little room where she was going to change into a brand-new, beautifully laundered white linen suit to wear to an upcoming appointment. As she was walking by the girl with the cocoa, Christine admonished her, "You had better be careful. You are going to spill that cocoa, the way that you are stirring it."

"Oh, no," replied the girl. Christine went on her way, changed her clothes, and returned to the stove for her daily cup. Just as Christine approached the stove, her co-worker gave one last wild turn with the spoon, tipping over the pot of cocoa, spilling it onto Christine's suit. Down to the hem the dark liquid ran.

The girl was terrified, remembering other outbursts of Christine's temper. She cried out, "Don't hit me — don't put the bowl over my head! I didn't mean to do it!"

For one split second, as it has been recounted by Christine so many times, she felt like hitting the girl with the spoon, putting the pan over her head, and giving her a good scolding. Suddenly Christine realized that things were different now, and rather than seeing an outburst, the girl heard Christine say, "You have done a careless thing, but I am not going to hit you, nor put the pot over your head."

Christine realized right there that God was doing a beautiful work of sanctification in her life. She has related that never again in that office, nor in any other place, did she have wild outbursts of temper. The girls in the office took special note of this change in Christine.

Conversion also made a difference in Christine's ability to trust in God for provision and direction. Christine knew that she must pay her debts. She had one very large debt which she had been unable to pay. Week after week she received the bill, and one day Christine took this need to God. She prayed, "God, we read in your Word that you will take care of our needs. Now, I need money to pay this debt." She then turned to her Bible, not really knowing the Word of God too well at that time. She opened it to Job 22:25 which reads, "Yea, the Almighty shall be thy defense, and thou shalt have plenty of silver." Taking this word for herself, Christine said, "Thank you, Lord."

She had a small concertina in her possession which she took to a local store, asking the proprietor to advertise it for sale. "Yes," he replied, "though there isn't much call for concertinas. However, I will do it." Christine thanked him and went on her way. Every day for several days, she either called him on the phone or stopped by, checking to see if the instrument had been sold. However, no one had purchased it.

Finally the day came when Christine was ordered by her creditor to pay the debt she owed. She arose that morning, quoted the Scripture that God had given her, and went to work. At noontime Christine walked to the store where the instrument had been left and asked Mr. Brown once more, "Have you sold my concertina yet?" While asking, her eyes scanned the store and she could not see it.

He replied, "Yes, I have just sold it, and a very strange thing happened: The individual who purchased it paid for it, all in silver." This is just what the Lord told Christine would happen — "Thou shalt have plenty of silver."

From that day on, Christine began to learn the life of faith, not only in monetary matters, but in every facet of her life. She went to the Lord, and she went to His Word. I personally can vouch that once she received an anointing from His Word, you could not make her faith waver. This was her way of life until she went to live with the One who had supplied all of her needs as she daily lived a life of faith here on earth.

Not only was her temper taken care of through conversion, and not only did she begin a life of faith and trust, but she also began to have tolerance toward the weaknesses and failures of others. The following story illustrates this quality in her life.

One day a group of people, Christine included, was sitting around a table when Christine observed one particular girl who seemed quite crude. She wasn't handling her silverware properly, and she was talking quite loudly, among other things. Christine took it upon herself to speak to her about it, and was quite sharp and curt with her words. The girl, Mabel, was very hurt by Christine's words and rushed from the table. "There," Christine said to herself, "she'll not do that again!"

A few days later, this same group was sitting around a table eating, when Christine spoke out of turn. Her pastor and head of the mission house, Rev. Penney, whom Christine greatly admired, admonished her that she was speaking out of turn and asked her to be quiet. She felt so humiliated before the people that her eyes filled with tears. She rose, ran to her room, and threw herself across her bed, crying her heart out.

In a few minutes she felt a tender tap on her shoulder, and looking up, she saw Mabel who said, "I knew I would find you here. This is exactly where I came the other day when your words hurt me so much." The girls forgave each other, cried a bit, and learned a very, very important lesson of the Christian life. Christine, as a babe in Christ, was growing in God.

Two years passed, and one day during a service at the mission church, the people were informed that a certain missionary, who had been working deep in the jungles of the Essequibo River with South American Indians, was ill and was being brought back to the mission station. The call went out for a man to take his place and continue the work among the Indians of the jungle. After this service ended, Christine went to Brother Penney and said, "I am offering myself for the missionary service in the Essequibo region."

"Oh, no, my dear," he replied, "that is no place for a young girl alone. I will not give my permission for you to go."

A few weeks passed, during which pleas were again made for a man to fill the sick missionary's place. Christine could be quiet no longer. She again went to her pastor and offered her services on the mission field. To this he replied, "Well, no one else has offered and you seem to have a definite calling. You may go!"

Christine offered her life in consecration to God, and left for the mission station in the interior jungles of British Guiana. She lived in a most primitive style, in a little hut that had a mud floor. She heard pigs and piglets squealing and screaming at night as huge anacondas came into the compound. Yes, she was nervous at times, she recalled, but she was also blessed, because many souls were saved through her ministry. Today a church stands in that part of the world as the result of her untiring labors there.

A Portuguese family owned a home and operated a store in the interior and Christine became acquainted with them. She witnessed to the woman, Mrs. Deswitt, who subsequently received Jesus Christ as her Savior.

This lady had compassion on the young missionary and said, "You can't live in that hut any more. I am going to take you into my home and I want you to live there and eat there. Let it be your home." Christine moved in and lived there until shortly after she was stricken with malaria fever.

Sister Gibson wrote of this terrible time of suffering, and the remarkable healing that she received from God. The Lord revealed to her, as she was lying on her bed of sickness, that her work at the station was about to end. She told this to some of the people there and they refused to believe that God would remove her from their midst. Their argument was that God could heal her there just as well as He could heal her in some other place.

She loved her work there and she loved the people — they were dear to her heart. Hence, she listened to their pleas and did not write to headquarters, asking for her removal. Earnest prayers ascended to God on her behalf, but to no avail. Stubbornly, the fever continued until she became so weak that she could not walk without help, and was finally confined to her bed. Her case became critical. She was advised to take quinine, the drug that was given for malaria fever. However, she had placed herself in God's hands for healing, and she refused this drug. Day and night she suffered with vomiting, chills, and fever until her vitality was so sapped that she looked like a skeleton.

The people finally became alarmed and felt that the officials of the mission should be notified. She knew that this was the right thing to do and felt that arrangements should be made for her immediate removal. It looked as though she would die and be buried there if this was not quickly done.

The day after the letter was sent to headquarters she picked up her Bible which was laying beside her on the bed, and felt impressed that God had a word for her. She waited for the Spirit to guide her in her reading, and she felt led to turn to the book of Ezekiel. She opened to the eighteenth chapter and read these words: "For I have no pleasure in the death of him that dieth, said the Lord God; wherefore turn yourselves and live." The words in the 32nd verse, "turn yourselves and live," went through her like a fire. She knew then that she would not die there.

At that time she was alone upstairs. Mrs. Deswitt had gone downstairs to help in the variety store. After this special word from God, Christine arose from her sick bed, put on her dressing gown and slippers, and started to walk. She was so weak that she fell to the floor two or three times but got up again and finally arrived downstairs. She feebly walked to the back of the store, determined to exercise her faith to "turn herself and live." As she stood at the door, Mrs. Deswitt turned from the counter and seeing her, began to scream almost hysterically. This lady, who had not overcome the ungodly superstitions that she had been taught in her country, screamed out loudly, "Christine has died and her spirit has come down to the store!"

"No, my dear," Christine replied, "I have not died. I may look like a ghost, but I am flesh, blood, and bones, and not a ghost. I have heard from the Lord. I am going to live!"

The people were indeed pleased that God had at last answered their prayers, and they again hoped that she would quickly regain her health and remain with them. This, however, was not to be, for God had other plans for Christine's life. Yes, "Zion, the joy of the whole earth," had to come into being, and Christine Eckman, chosen of God as a vessel prepared for the Master's use, was now ready to obey the further leadings of her Lord and say goodbye to these friends. They wept as the time of her departure drew near, but she commended them to God and the Word of His grace, knowing that He would take care of them and provide another missionary to take her place. "To obey is better than sacrifice, and to hearken, than the fat of rams" (1 Sam. 15:22).

She made preparations to be taken down the river in a dugout and to meet the steamer which would take her back to Georgetown. God had miraculously healed her, but she was very weakened from this siege of malaria.

When Christine got back to the mission station, she spent about two weeks in bed recuperating, before she was strong enough to get up and walk around the mission grounds. She was tested a few times with symptoms of malaria, but her faith never wavered. She knew that God had given His word to her and that He had no pleasure in her death. After each attack, she "turned herself to live." Satan knew that he could not defeat her, and after a short while, the sickness disappeared. Malaria fever seldom leaves a body in a hurry, but God so miraculously healed her that after those few times of testing, she was completely delivered and had no return of malaria fever from that time on.

> There is a healing branch that grows
> Where every bitter Marah flows,
> This is our health-reviving tree —
> "I am the Lord that healeth thee."
>
> There is an old appointed way
> For those who "hearken and obey"
> Above the gale these words we see
> "I am the Lord that healeth thee."
>
> There is a Great Physician still
> Whose hand has all its ancient skill;
> At His command, our pains will flee;
> "I am the Lord that healeth thee."
>
> (Selected)

Chapter 3
Not Knowing Whither She Went

"By faith Abraham...went out, not knowing whither he went"
(Heb. 11:8).

While Christine was at the mission, she became acquainted with an American missionary lady who was preparing to leave shortly for America, to visit her brother in San Jose, California. Her husband was remaining on the mission field while she went to America.

This lady noticed the frailty of the little missionary who had just returned from the jungles and invited her to travel to America with her. She felt that a sea voyage would be just the thing to rejuvenate Christine after such a severe illness. She also promised to stir up the interest of the mission church for Christine's passage money. This she did.

All this seemed like the providence of God, for Christine was still in a weakened condition physically and would not be able to do missionary work for a while. Christine felt it was God's will for her to go to America. She expected that they would be gone for only a few months and then return, since the missionary lady was leaving her husband on the mission field. Christine was also pleased with the thought of seeing the United States of America, the land of which she had heard so much. In spite of all this, in the plan of God, Christine was never to return to her homeland of South America.

At about the same time that Christine received the invitation to go to the United States, she received a letter from Rev. Reuben

Gibson. He stated that he had never forgotten her, and that the Lord had opened the way for him to take a trip with a party of Christian and Missionary Alliance missionaries. The party intended to visit a number of mission stations and would be visiting the one he had left many months before. His letter also stated that he was looking forward, with much joy, to seeing her again and would have much to say to her. This letter greatly disturbed her peace, for she didn't especially want to see him again, remembering the circumstances connected with his leaving Georgetown.

In comparing dates, Christine noted that, indeed, their boats would pass each other on the wide, wide seas. She concluded then that he would not see her, for was she not on her way to California? And was she not returning later to South America? Yes, so she thought, but man's ways are not God's ways, for God's "ways are past finding out." (See Romans 11:33.)

Truly God bringeth the blind by a way that they knew not and leadeth them in paths that they have not known. (See Isaiah 42:16.)

This verse proved true of Christine. She was indeed blind as to the future. Unknowingly, she had more than one reason for leaving her homeland and taking the voyage to America.

The day finally arrived when she said goodbye to friends and loved ones and the voyage began. The missionary lady was very jubilant that day, but Christine's heart felt a little fearful and sad. She was leaving her homeland for the first time. She was also leaving her beloved sister Alice, and a number of Christian friends. She was starting out for an unknown country, and she would surely find herself among strangers. All this gave her an uneasy feeling as the steamer left the shores of South America. However, she committed herself to God and felt that He would protect her from all danger.

Everything went well until they reached Jamaica, British West Indies. Here the boat stopped to take on passengers, and among those who came on board was a very distinguished-looking gentleman. She learned that he was an American businessman in charge of a large fruit concern in Jamaica.

In a day or two he became very friendly with Christine and her missionary friend, and it did not take Christine long to see that her friend was captivated by him. They became so "over-friendly" that when the two ladies were alone in their berth, Christine took her to task about the matter. Christine reminded her that she was a married woman and that she had left her husband in the work of the Lord. What an awakening Christine then received!

The woman informed Christine that she had "left that old man for good," referring to her husband. Indeed, he was many years her elder. The friend went on to fill Christine's ears with words and comments that cannot be repeated in this book. Christine was horrified. The woman then informed her that she never intended to return to the mission field, and had seen her husband for the last time. Seeing the shocked look on Christine's face, the woman tried to pacify her. She told Christine that she, of course, would see about getting Christine back to her homeland and mission work, and then admonished her, "Don't look so scared."

Scared she was, though, for she wondered that was coming next and what she could do without money and with no one to whom she could turn if things should get worse. She earnestly prayed that night for God to undertake and to make His will known to her. Christine found out later, through the captain, that the woman had registered on the boat as a widow.

For days things did not go very smoothly between the two women. Christine tried to do a little missionary work aboard the boat, but soon saw that it was displeasing to the former missionary and her gentleman friend. He, however, was quite a diplomat and showed no resentment when she talked to him regarding his soul's salvation. Instead, he laughed at her and called her a "Puritan." And so it went until they reached New York City.

> O God, our help in ages past,
> Our hope for years to come,
> Our shelter from the stormy blast,
> And our eternal home.
>
> (Isaac Watts)

> Under the shadow of Thy throne,
> Still may we dwell secure;
> Sufficient is thine arm alone,
> And our defense is sure.

> A thousand ages, in Thy sight,
> Are like an evening gone;
> Short as the watch that ends the night,
> Before the rising sun.
>
> (Selected)

Chapter 4
Deliverance From a Snare

> "For he looked for a city which hath foundations, whose builder and maker is God"
> (Heb. 11:10).

The following is taken directly from Sister Gibson's personal writings:

We had come to the end of the sea voyage. The big city, New York, was in sight. Yes, we had arrived at last. Here was New York City with its teeming multitudes, vehicles running to and fro, massive buildings and high towers, but could we say of New York: "whose builder and maker is God"! I think not — even though the gentleman kept telling me that we had arrived in "God's Country," meaning the United States of America.

America is indeed a wonderful country, and it has become to me the land of my adoption as far as an earthly home can be. However, is it the city Abraham looked for, whose builder and maker is God? I think differently about New York City or any of the large cities in America. The city that Abraham looked for is described as a "heavenly place." It is a country where no sickness, poverty, or heartaches shall exist. Its builder and maker is truly God, our Savior, and it is being prepared for those of like precious faith with Abraham. The heavenly Jerusalem

— that is the city I am bound for — the home prepared for the bride, the Lamb's wife.

I love to think that there is such a future home for the saints of God, but let me come back to earth for the present, and continue my story.

Here we were in the midst of much excitement. Our gentleman friend, whom I shall name Mr. X, proved a great help to us in seeing us through customs, explaining things to various officials for us, taking care of our baggage, etc. I was so nervous and half-scared, that I hardly knew what was going on until I found myself with my missionary friend and Mr. X in a large hotel somewhere in Brooklyn, New York. My missionary friend assured me that there was nothing to worry about — Mr. X, this kind gentleman, would take care of everything for us.

A bellboy took our luggage and we were ushered into a suite of rooms with a bath, etc. I was informed that we would stay here until we were rested and the plans for our next move had been decided.

I thought I had struck fairyland! At the same time, I was wondering where all this would end. Mr. X took a room on the opposite side of ours, and it looked as though he had become one of us.

It was late afternoon when we reached the hotel. I was very tired and hungry, even though we had lunched earlier in the day. It was understood that we were to meet Mr. X in the hotel lobby and dine with him in the hotel dining room that evening.

I took out my simple, navy-blue dress with a white collar to wear, for all my dresses were that style.

My missionary friend informed me that she was not going down to the dining hall with the kind of dresses she then possessed. Furthermore, she was very exhausted and had a severe headache. I would have to meet Mr. X and keep the appointment with him. She said she would meet him later and go for a walk with him. Imagine my embarrassment at having to meet this man alone and dine with him! My missionary friend was very insistent that I meet the appointment, and not offend Mr. X. I was rather hungry, so obediently I wended my way down to the lobby and met him. My embarrassment became greater when I saw him in evening dress.

The dining hall was brilliantly lighted, and turning to him, I inquired, "Are you not ashamed of me?" Laughingly, he answered, "Oh, no, Puritan, I am proud of you. This is America. We do as we please. Come along with me."

I gave him the message from my missionary friend and entered the dining hall by his side. We sat at a table for two. I can hardly remember now all the good things we ate, but the food was delicious. My companion was very pleasant and helped me to relax. While I sat there, my mind kept wandering off to my friend [Rev. Reuben Gibson] and the missionaries who left [America] about the same time that we left for the U.S.A. Something told me that he was still in this country. I felt that I should send him a telegram and get in touch with him. Mr. X then said, 'Why don't you do it?' I replied, 'I don't know how far it is from New York City, and the cost of sending such a telegram.' The truth was, I did not have the money.

"Oh," said Mr. X, "don't worry about the cost. I will take care of that for you."

After dinner we went to the telegraph office in the hotel. I wrote a telegram stating that I was in New York at the Brooklyn Hotel, and would like to see him there. This was just the opposite of what I had felt when leaving British Guiana. Here I was doing the very thing that I was avoiding when I left my homeland — asking to see the person I had been afraid to meet when he wrote that he was returning to the mission field. Had I gone mental? After the telegram was sent, I became quite perturbed. After thanking him for his kindness, I bade Mr. X good night and left him in the lobby where he said he would await the missionary.

As I entered the room, she was all dressed and said to me, "Lock yourself in and go to bed. We may not be back until very late."

Oh, what a night I spent! I prostrated myself on the floor and wept before God. After a while, my spirit became quiet, and I must have fallen asleep, for it was after midnight when I was awakened by my missionary friend coming in. She seemed to be elated and began to tell me abut the plans they had made. We were to travel with Mr. X, and he was taking us to the World's Fair in St. Louis, Missouri. She said that they were going to give me a wonderful time, and that I would see a good many places before we reached California. Oh, how my heart trembled at all this talk! The more she rambled on, the stronger I felt that this was not God's plan for me, and that He was going to deliver me from this snare.

Deliverance From a Snare

My missionary friend seemed so worldly minded. I could hardly believe that she was the same person whom I knew in the South American mission. I breathed a prayer that early morning to my God, and felt the assurance that He was silently planning for me.

> He leadeth me: O blessed thought!
> O words with heav'nly comfort fraught!
> What-e'er I do, where-e're I be,
> Still 'tis God's hand that leadeth me.
>
> Lord, I would clasp thy hand in mine
> Nor ever murmur nor repine,
> Content, whatever lot I see,
> Since 'tis my God that leadeth me.
>
> He leadeth me, He leadeth me,
> By His own hand He leadeth me;
> His faithful foll'wer I would be,
> For by His hand He leadeth me.
>
> (Joseph H. Gilmore)

Chapter 5
I Being in the Way, the Lord Led Me

> "I [the servant] being in the way, the Lord led me"
> (Gen. 24:27).

Sister Gibson continues her story:

Yes, strange and varied have been the leadings of the Lord in my life, but I know that His way is always the right way; and thus it has proved with me.

As I arose that next morning and began dressing, my thoughts wandered to the night before — the dinner with Mr. X, and that urge to send a telegram to my preacher friend [Rev. Reuben Gibson]. I had sent the telegram, and now questions flooded my mind. Did he receive that telegram? Will I receive an answer today? Is he really in this country? Am I deluded?

The answer to my questions was not long in coming. A knock on our door and the voice of a bellboy announcing a telegram for Miss Eckman aroused me from my reverie. My missionary friend was surprised, and of course, it necessitated some explaining to her.

My heart was throbbing and my hands were trembling as I opened the envelope and read the telegram. It read: "Leaving on midnight train. Will be with you in the morning."

And so it came to pass that my preacher friend, [Rev. Reuben Gibson] and I stood facing each other in the hotel drawing room later that day, hardly knowing what to say for a few minutes. He broke the silence with these words, "Christine, what are you doing here, and why have you sent for me?"

These questions gave me an opportunity to explain everything. I was curious to know why he had not gone on his missionary tour according to the date stated in his letter to me. As he related the circumstances that had delayed the party from leaving the country until a week or two later, we both saw that there was a peculiar providence of God in the whole affair. Even though we were somewhat bewildered as to the meaning of it all, we were very conscious that the Lord had a plan for our lives and would make it clear to us.

Rev. Gibson proposed to Christine that day, asking her to marry him. He suggested that together they could go into the work of the Lord. However, Christine declined this invitation to marry.

We go on with her story here:

I also found out that sometime during the past years he and my missionary friend had met, and so it was not as difficult as I thought to get them together. He was very tender and sympathetic with her as he endeavored to persuade her to change her plans and separate from Mr. X.

He tried to show her that, as a Christian, she surely could not have fellowship with a worldly businessman, and go traveling around the country with him. Then, when we found that nothing could dissuade her from her purpose to have Mr. X as her companion, and that her mind was fully made up, I realized that a problem was facing me.

If I did not continue with them, I would have to seek help from my preacher friend. He had earlier made a proposition to me, but I had refused it, as some things were not clear to me. O, what a dilemma I seemed to be in!

My missionary friend became very provoked with me, and began to accuse me of disloyalty to her. It was a tense moment for all of us. I was torn between my feelings of obligation to her for all she had done in taking care of my expenses thus far, and my loyalty to God, to separate from that which I knew was wrong. Then, here was my preacher friend offering me his love and protection, and yet I could not feel free to accept his proposal even though I knew that God was in his coming to meet me.

We three sat in that hotel room for several minutes without talking. I was earnestly praying for light as to the next move. Suddenly my preacher friend exclaimed, "I believe God has shown me what to do for you, Christine."

He then told me that he had some very dear friends in East Providence, Rhode Island. They were a married couple in charge of a Faith Home, and had been on the mission field some years before. He knew that they would be glad to accommodate me in the home, as they were still interested in missionary work. He said that he would take me there, and I could stay with them until I was shown clearly what to do.

When Christine heard him say "Rhode Island," she thought immediately that it would be another boat trip. However, it was explained that she would be able to go there by train.

We pick up Christine's story again:

> My missionary friend was greatly perturbed and we had a rather difficult time to get my things from her, and leave the hotel, but there was nothing else to do. She would not hear of separating from Mr. X, and I was sure that God did not want me to continue traveling with them. Arrangements were made and later my preacher friend and I took the train for Providence, Rhode Island.
>
> The date of my arrival in Faith Home was in the month of October, 1905. My friend [Rev. Reuben Gibson] introduced me to Brother and Sister Thomas Crocker and they gave me a very warm welcome. I learned that this was a home for elderly people, but was glad to know that the Crockers had a young daughter, Alice, a very pleasant girl. I felt that my friendship with her would help take away some of the loneliness I expected to experience in the days to come.
>
> My preacher friend had to leave the next day for his home in Foxboro, Massachusetts, but promised to return and see me before leaving for his missionary tour. He again urged me to reconsider his offer, stating that if I would do so, he would change his plans about leaving the country, and make other arrangements for both of us.
>
> This was truly a temptation to me in my hour of perplexity, but I did not have the mind of God about

my future, and could not take this step in the dark. I asked him to be patient with me and to wait until we both knew definitely that it was God's will for us to be united. I also urged him to go on his missionary tour as he had planned, and give me time to think and pray about the future.

The day came when I had to bid him farewell. He had finally decided to take the missionary tour to the West Indies and South America. I did not see him again for two years.

>Lead, kindly Light, amid th' encircling gloom,
>   Lead Thou me on!
>The night is dark, and I am far from home;
>   Lead Thou me on!
>Keep Thou my feet; I do not ask to see
>The distant scene; one step enough for me.
>
>So long Thy pow'r hath blest me,
>   Sure it still will lead me on.
>O'er moor and fen, o'er crag and torrent, till
>   The night is gone,
>And with the morn those angel faces smile
>Which I have loved long since, and lost awhile!
>
>   (John Henry Newman)

Chapter 6
Not You.... But God

"So now it was not you that sent me hither, but God" (Gen. 45:8).

Sister Gibson's story continues:

These words [above] were spoken by Joseph at the time when he revealed himself to his brethren, and they are surely recorded for our benefit and blessing. How strange are the providences of God! Truly, "His ways are past finding out." In the beginning, it looked as though Joseph's being in Egypt was the direct result of his brothers' hatred. (See Genesis 37:28.) "And they...sold Joseph to the Ishmaelites for twenty pieces of silver: and they brought Joseph into Egypt."

But afterwards! "What I do thou knowest not now, but thou shalt know hereafter" (John 13:7). Ah, yes, there is surely an afterward in all God's dealings. Let us be patient with our God. He knows how to make "all things work together for good to them that love God and are the called according to His purpose." (See Romans 8:28.)

And so it was in my case. It looked in the beginning as though my leaving my homeland and taking that voyage with the missionary friend was all a mistake. Here I was, stranded in America, lonesome and perplexed. What was I doing in East Providence,

Rhode Island, in a home for the aged? Was it not through the doings of my missionary friend and that Mr. X? In the natural, yes, but today I can say with Joseph, "not you, but God." It was not their wrongdoing and my human mistake, as I at first thought, which accounted for what I was now facing. They were just the instruments whom God, in His permissive will, used to bring me into His purpose and plan, so that Zion could come into being and be "the joy of the whole earth."

The departure of my preacher friend on his missionary journey was just another link in God's providential chain in bringing me here. Now he was gone and I was left to find out just what my next step should be.

The Crockers were very kind to me. I had also become acquainted with Rev. and Mrs. Alpheus Angel Cleveland, an elderly couple who were then residing in Faith Home. I found out that Brother Cleveland was the founder of Faith Home, but had resigned as manager in favor of Brother Thomas Crocker, as he was not well and quite aged.

During my days of perplexity, Brother Cleveland was a great help to me as I found him to be a man of strong faith. Many were the stories he and his wife rehearsed to me of God's dealings with them in their life of faith when they were in charge of the home. Brother Cleveland was at this time pastoring a small Holiness assembly located a few blocks from Faith Home. He invited me to visit his church and speak to the people concerning my missionary work in South America. This I did on two or three occasions, and found the people very friendly toward me which helped dispel my gloom.

A few weeks later, I met a Quaker minister and his wife, Rev. and Mrs. Kimber. They invited me to their lovely home in Newport, Rhode Island [probably for the Christmas holidays], and while there, I was introduced to a number of ministers belonging to the Holiness group. Through them I received an invitation to attend a missionary conference to be held in God's Bible School in Cincinnati, Ohio. Thus began my first trip to the Middle West [probably in the spring of 1906].

The Kimbers took care of my expenses, and thinking that through this conference, the way might open for me to return to my missionary field in British Guiana, I was glad to accept the invitation. I went to the conference and certainly enjoyed the fellowship of those dear people and felt the presence of God in the meetings.

I met a Rev. and Mrs. Crawford during the conference who became very friendly with me, and after hearing my story, invited me to travel with them. They were evangelists and had many open doors. They felt sure that I would receive opportunities to speak in their campaigns, and receive offerings which would enable me to return to my homeland and my field of labor.

I visited several places with these dear people, and had a variety of peculiar experiences — some rather unpleasant ones, as well as those that were more favorable. However, God never allowed me to receive enough money to pay my fare back to the West Indies and South America.

After being with them for several months, and meeting a host of friends among the Holiness people and the Christian and Missionary Alliance people in Indianapolis, Indiana, and other places, I began to feel very strongly that I should return to the Faith Home of East Providence, Rhode Island. I wrote the Crockers, asking permission to return, and after receiving a favorable answer, I did so. I had just enough money to pay my train fare and buy something to eat on the journey [probably during the winter of 1906/7].

GOD MEANT IT UNTO GOOD
(Genesis 50:20)

"God meant it unto good" — O blest assurance,
    Falling like sunshine all across life's way,
Touching with Heaven's gold, earth's darkest storm clouds,
    Bringing fresh peace and comfort day by day.

'Twas not by chance the hands of faithless brethren
    Sold Joseph captive to a foreign land;
Nor was it chance which, after years of suffering,
    Brought him before the monarch's throne to stand.

One Eye all-seeing saw the need of thousands,
    And planned to meet it through that one lone soul;
And through the weary days of prison bondage
    Was working towards the great and glorious goal.

As yet the end was hidden from the captive,
    The iron entered even to his soul;
His eye could scan the present path of sorrow,
    Nor yet his gaze might rest upon the whole.

Not You . . . . But God

Faith failed not through those long, dark days of waiting,
    His trust in God was recompensed at last,
The moment came when God led forth His servant
    To succour many, all his sufferings past.

"It was not you, but God, that sent me hither."
    Witnessed triumphant faith in after days;
God meant it unto good, "no second causes"
    Mingled their discord with his song of praise.

"God meant it unto good" for thee, beloved,
    The God of Joseph is the same today;
His love permits afflictions strange and bitter,
    His hand is guiding through the unknown way.

Thy Lord, who sees the end from the beginning
    Hath purposes for thee of Love untold.
Then place thy hand in His and follow fearless,
    Till thou the riches of His grace behold.

There, when thou standest in the Home of Glory,
    And all life's path lies open to thy gaze,
Thine eyes shall see the hand which now thou trustest,
    And magnify His love through endless days.

                (Freda Hanbury Allen)

Chapter 7
Visions and Revelations

"Where there is no vision, the people perish" (Prov. 29:18).

Sister Gibson's story continues to unfold:

We must always remember that visions have their appointed time and some of God's dear children become very impatient in waiting for the vision to speak. See Hebrews 10:35 — "and some even cast away their confidence which hath a great recompense of reward."

The days that followed my return to the Faith Home at East Providence were truly days of severe testing, but God was faithful and held me steady although the "trial of faith" continued for some time.

The first test that I met with on my return to the Home was, "No room in the inn." I was informed that every bedroom was occupied and I would have to sleep on a couch in the Crockers' living room for the present. This was very embarrassing, as Mr. Crocker had to pass through the room in the early mornings to attend to his duties. A folding screen had been placed around the couch to protect me from view, but I was very conscious that I was in the way.

I had not been in the home many days when the Crockers approached me about returning to the mission field. They informed me that one of the executives of the Missionary Board was available and that they would get in touch with him if I so desired. They assured me that he would give me the proper advice and might even provide the fare for my passage back to the field. I was glad for this information and consented to see him.

In a few days he arrived, but his interview with me was very unfavorable. He bluntly told me not to expect any money from the Missionary Board, as they were not responsible for my coming to America, and if I felt that God wanted me back on the mission field, I would have to look to Him alone to get me there. He was so severe in his talk that I regretted giving my consent to meet him, and I was not sorry to see him depart.

After I was left alone, I threw myself upon the couch where I had been sleeping and wept bitterly. I wondered if "God had forgotten to be gracious." I felt that "No man cared for my soul." Oh, how often we human beings misjudge and misunderstand the providences of our God.

I had been lying there only a short time when I heard the still, small voice of my Lord. It came so tenderly to my inner being, *"My child, thou art not forsaken"; "Cast not away thy confidence"; "I am working for thee"; "I will show thee some of my future plans."* Immediately my spirit was quieted, and I seemed to be carried out of myself. I looked and beheld on the wall of my room something like a white screen. It seemed I was about to see moving pictures. Scene after scene was shown to me. I will just relate the first one.

I saw a large hall with chairs and a platform and other furniture. A Voice said to me, *"This is the mission church of Alpheus Angel Cleveland."* I remembered the hall, as I had spoken there once before I left for the West. The Voice continued, *"You will be called to fill Alpheus Cleveland's place as pastor. He is going to resign shortly, and you will be his successor."*

That picture left the screen and others began to appear in succession. When I came to myself, I realized that I had seen a vision and wondered what it all meant. I sat for some time on the couch, startled and almost frightened. I wondered if God was really showing me my future, or was I being deluded by Satan? I began to earnestly pray that God would keep me in my right mind and not let me be deceived by the devil. I promised then and there that I would tell the vision to no one, but would watch and wait for it *to speak*. Then, I would not risk being put to shame by *believing a lie*.

The day after all this had transpired, Brother Cleveland met me in the hallway and invited me to his room. After some conversation, he asked me to speak at their mid-week meeting in the mission church. The church was located in a hall just a few blocks from the Faith Home. I was glad to accept the invitation and get my mind on something other than the occurrence of the day before.

When we entered the hall that night, how forcibly that first scene stood before me! Here was the hall and the furniture just as I beheld them in the vision. In that service the Lord made me a blessing to the people, and at the close of the meeting, they requested

Brother Cleveland to continue the services for that week and have me as the speaker, which he did. Thus began a series of evangelistic meetings which finally led to the fulfillment of my first vision.

There shall be a performance of those things,
That loving heart hath waited long to see —
Those words shall be fulfilled to which she clings,
Because her God hath promised faithfully;

And knowing Him, she ne'er can doubt His word,
He speaks, and it is done, the mighty Lord.
There shall be a performance of those things,
O trusting heart, the Lord to thee hath told.

Let Faith and Hope arise, and plume their wings,
And soar towards the sunrise clouds of gold;
The portals of the rosy dawn swing aside,
Revealing joys the darkening night did hide.

(Selected)

Chapter 8
Your Life Is Hidden With Christ in God

"It is not expedient for me, doubtless, to glory. I will come to visions and revelations of the Lord"
(2 Cor. 12:1).

Sister Gibson's story continues:

At this time I will deviate a little, as I wish to include an incident which occurred during my visit to the Middle West [c. 1906]. I was in the city of Indianapolis, Indiana, where I was staying with my friends, Brother and Sister Crawford.

May God use what is about to be related to help those who, like myself, may be seeking light on deeper lines of truth. Also, that He will make my friends understand that my chief reason for giving it here is this: *Because the revelation has played such an important part in God's dealings with me during the past years, I feel that it belongs in the story of my life.*

During those days in the Middle West, I was thrown in with several Holiness preachers, the Crawfords being evangelists with that group, and I myself being associated in missionary work among the Holiness people. I heard much preaching about "dying to self," the "death route" being one of their special lines of teaching. My heart was hungry for a deeper experience in God, but I saw very little practical demonstration in their daily living, of the very truth which they were preaching. I was becoming rather skeptical, until God in His love and mercy took me in hand and revealed what I am about to write in this chapter.

It began one day while I was reading the Epistle of Paul to the Colossians (Col. 3:3,4). I stopped and began to meditate on those verses. "For ye are dead, and your life is hidden with Christ in God. When Christ, Who is our life, shall appear, then shall ye also appear with Him in glory."

Here I was facing the same line of teaching I had so often heard preached, but did not comprehend. I asked then that the Holy Spirit would guide me into this truth, and remove my doubts and fears. God took me at my word, and the next day placed a desire in my heart to shut myself in with Him. I obtained permission from Sister Crawford to exempt myself from meals and company.

O, what a day that was! Never can I wholly forget what I realized in that revelation of biblical truth. When I entered the bedroom and knelt beside a chair, I was very conscious that I was entering into the "Holy of Holies." My soul was deeply stirred in prayer. Then a stillness crept over me, and I felt that I was about to be shown the true meaning of the Scripture I had read the day before. And so it came to pass.

In a vision I entered Gethsemane, and was about to drink a cup that was very distasteful to me. I found myself saying, "O Lord, let this cup pass from me."

An agony of intense suffering came over me, but my spirit was quieted when I was told by an inner voice, *"Child, you are fellowshipping the sufferings of Christ. You are not alone. I am taking you through."* Then I began to repeat, "Not my will, but Thine be done."

This went on for some time, and then I sensed I was about to be taken through the Crucifixion. I felt the pain of nails piercing my hands and feet. Again, I was shrinking from disgrace and humiliation connected with the cross, but the tender voice of Jesus quieted every nerve, and a sweet peace took possession of me.

He assured me that I was being made comfortable to His death, and that He would never leave me nor forsake me. What a yieldedness entered my being! I began to feel that it was an honor, rather than a disgrace, to share His sufferings on the cross. Yes, I saw myself hanging there; I heard the slanderous talk of those watching me die. Some were criticizing my life, while others were praising my virtues, telling of all the service I had accomplished for my Lord, etc. and although I knew it was I hanging on that cross, I was looking at the dead figure hanging there, from whom no response was coming, and in whom not even a muscle was moving.

I found myself saying, "She is dead, she is dead." Then I realized that I was going to be buried. I was lowered into an open grave and a horror of darkness swept over me. This lasted for a while, after which that scene changed and I heard voices saying, "The resurrection morning has come." I expected to see myself emerge from the grave, but to my amazement, a man came forth and I saw Jesus. I cried out, "Where am I?" And the answer came, *"Your life is hidden with Christ in God."*

Then I came to myself and realized that I had just passed through — in vision — the true meaning of the teaching I had so desired to understand. I sat in my room for hours, awed by the presence of the Lord. Something had really happened to me, and although I knew very little at that time about the Pentecostal way, I do believe that I was under a spiritual anointing. My whole being seemed to be filled with the Divine Presence, and these words were going through me, "When Christ, Who is our life shall appear, then shall you also appear with Him in glory" (Col. 3:4). I made a deeper consecration in my room that day and promised my Lord that, by His grace, I would go forth, taking a "death route."

Many years have passed since then, and I have met with the reality of the revelation shown me that day in a variety of ways.

Chapter 9
With God Nothing Shall Be Impossible

"My brethren, count it all joy when ye fall into divers temptations; knowing this, that the trying of your faith worketh patience"
(James 1:2,3).

In the last chapter, we related a vision that Sister Christine received as she visited in the Midwest [c. 1906], and now we continue the story of her life.

She had been invited to conduct a series of evangelistic services for the Rev. Alpheus Cleveland in East Providence, Rhode Island [probably during the fall of 1907]. These meetings had been held for but a few evenings when an interruption occurred.

One morning Brother Cleveland called her into his room to introduce her to a preacher. Brother Cleveland explained that this gentleman was an evangelist who had previously written to him, requesting the opportunity to come and conduct some meetings. Brother Cleveland had written back, inviting the man to come. However, Brother Cleveland had forgotten the dates involved. The evangelist had come, expecting to begin his meetings right away.

Brother Cleveland then began to explain to him that evangelistic meetings being held at the time were progressing well under Sister Christine's ministry, and wondered if maybe they could work together for a while. Oh, what a look came over that man's face as he said, "Excuse me, Brother Cleveland, but I do not care to have a woman assist me in my meetings. I am capable of conducting my campaigns alone!"

Christine was certain that she would be dismissed. It staggered her for a moment, for God was truly blessing the services and her ministry there. She was sure that her first vision was going to be fulfilled. What a temptation to doubt! Yes, she had "fallen into temptation" and her heart felt sorrowful. It was, however, only for a moment, for God quickly brought the Scripture to her mind, "Count it all joy when ye fall into divers temptations; knowing this, that the trying of your faith worketh patience" (James 1:2,3).

She realized that this was only "the trying of her faith." She then assured Brother Cleveland that he was welcome to continue the meetings with this evangelist, since he had invited him for those particular dates. She told him that she would take her place in the congregation and would help in prayer for the success of the services. Sister Gibson later remarked, "Poor Brother Cleveland — he was so terribly embarrassed." Christine tried to forget her own disappointment and focused on comforting him all that she could.

The meetings continued, with the new evangelist as the speaker. Brother Cleveland invited Christine to the platform and asked her to pray. However, the evangelist totally ignored her and the meetings seemed to lose their former vitality and spirit. Christine sensed that her presence was annoying him. Consequently, rather than hinder the services, she absented herself from the church during his campaign.

The last night of the meetings, Brother Cleveland called a business meeting and tendered his resignation. Christine was not present but was told by some of the members that the evangelist had spoken to some of them, saying that he would be very happy to fill Brother Cleveland's place as pastor, and that he hoped that they would choose to have him. Christine knew then why the visiting evangelist did not want her around. She did not have to wait very long to find out what had occurred at the business meeting.

Later Brother Cleveland sent for her and as she entered his room, he said, "Has God shown you anything?"

"What do you mean?" questioned Christine.

"I mean concerning your future."

"Well, Brother Cleveland, that is a secret between God and me," Christine explained.

Just previous to this, Christine had begun to pack her trunk, preparing to return to South America to resume her missionary work. However, as she was packing, she heard an inner voice tell her that she would never return to her native land and that she would stay in North America — in fact, in East Providence, Rhode Island, and would become the successor to Rev. Cleveland. She had difficulty believing or accepting that word from the Lord; however, when he called her into the room, she knew for sure that it was God who had spoken to her.

Brother Cleveland's face seemed to be illumined with the glory of God as he said, "I know that God has shown you that you are to be my successor." Christine started trembling in his presence. Was her vision really coming to pass?

Brother Cleveland placed his hands on her shoulders and said, "Don't be afraid to tell me."

Christine then asked, "Brother Cleveland, will you please tell me what God has revealed to you?"

As near as Sister Christine could remember, these are the words he said: "My child, you had not been in this house very long when my heavenly Father began to talk to me about you. I had been praying to be shown who the one was who should fill my place in the church, and also to carry out the vision that God had shown me for this work. I know that the time of my departure is at hand. I am aged and cannot continue my ministry. One day, as you passed my room, the Lord said to me, *'There is your successor.'* I answered with surprise, 'A woman, Lord?' I had thought that it would be a man, but 'God's ways are not ours, neither are His thoughts our thoughts.'

"Sister Eckman, you are not going back to the mission field. God has a work for you to do in America, and you must not fail Him." Continuing, Brother Cleveland said, "I have told my vision to my church, and there was a unanimous vote for you to take my place as pastor of The Church of the First Born."

> If we could see beyond today, as God can see;
> If all the clouds should roll away, the shadows flee;
> O'er present griefs we would not fret,
> Each sorrow we would soon forget,
> For many joys are waiting yet for you and me.
> If we could see, if we could know, we often say,
> But God in love a veil doth throw across our way;
> We cannot see what lies before,
> And so we cling to Him the more;
> He leads us till this life is o'er; trust and obey.
>   (Selected)

It was nearing the Christmas season [c. 1907], and as Sister Eckman began to consider what Brother Cleveland had suggested, questions arose in her mind: "How shall this be? Will the church be satisfied with a woman pastor? I have only done missionary work in a foreign country. Am I qualified to take charge of an American assembly?" Such questions greatly troubled her. She knew, however, that God had prepared her for this call through the vision, and that the vision was now speaking.

Christine relates:

> Brother Cleveland was so positive that God had spoken that I would be his successor, he just went ahead and made plans for my ordination to the ministry.

Just about this time, Christine's preacher friend had returned to America from his missionary tour and was now back at his pastorate in Foxboro, Massachusetts. To Christine's surprise, Brother Cleveland informed her that he had written to him about the ordination and invited him to officiate. Thus it came to pass that Rev. Reuben A. Gibson, pastor of the Christian and Missionary Alliance Church, preached her ordination sermon. He was one of the ministers who laid hands upon her and set her apart as pastor of The Church of the First Born. Strange indeed are the providences of our Lord!

> When it was understood that I would remain in this country, I wrote to my sister, Alice Dunn, and I would like to introduce her into this story, since she has played such an important part.

When Christine Eckman came to the United States, she left Alice with a family who were members of the Mission Church in South America. They corresponded regularly, and both of them felt that the Lord, in His own time, would bring them together again. Therefore, as soon as Christine knew that East Providence was to be her home for a while, she began making arrangements for Alice to come to America. God wonderfully provided the means for the voyage, and He brought Alice safely to the shores of the United States. She was always a blessing in the life of her sister and stood faithfully with her in the work of their precious Lord and Savior — the work that God entrusted Sister Gibson with for so many years.

After the resignation of the Rev. Alpheus A. Cleveland [c. spring 1908], and she took over the pastorate of The Church of the First Born, she was associated with a Holiness group. They taught sanctification as a second work of grace, a definite blessing to be sought for and received after conversion. She knew that God, in answer to her earnest prayers, had cleansed her heart of carnal desires and had given her the assurance of a sanctified life in Christ Jesus.

Time and time again, her thoughts went to Mary, the mother of Jesus. What a consecration Mary had which made possible the accomplishing of God's redemptive plan in the birth of His Son as the Savior of the world! Mary's example deeply influenced Christine's dedication to God.

Truly, God's ways are not our ways, neither are His thoughts our thoughts. In working out His plans, He confounds the wisdom of the wise and brings to naught the understanding of the prudent. The virgin Mary was greatly perturbed at her call of God unto motherhood. Her question to the angel Gabriel, who was sent with the message, showed her perplexity. "How shall this be?" (Luke 1:34). A virgin to bring forth a son? This was never heard of before. With God, however, nothing shall be impossible. And so it was with Christine Eckman. The call to Brother Cleveland's church began to arouse questions in her mind, but, as Mary of old, she could only say, "Be it unto me, according to Thy word" (Luke 1:38).

Chapter 10
This Is That Spoken by the Prophet Joel

"And it shall come to pass in the last days, saith God, I will pour out of my Spirit upon all flesh"
(Acts 2:17).

After Miss Eckman had been pastoring the church in East Providence for a period of time, she received an invitation to minister during a week of meetings that were to be held at a Holiness church in Massachusetts [probably in the fall of 1908].

Christine accepted the invitation and during her time there, the pastor of the church received a package in the mail. He opened it in her presence and exclaimed, "I wonder what fanatic sent these papers to me!" Christine asked what they were, and with disgust in his voice, he said, "These papers contain the erroneous doctrine of tongues as the evidence of the baptism of the Holy Ghost."

"Oh," cried Christine, "please let me read them!"

"Indeed not!" he replied. "I will never let you get into error. I shall burn the packet." This he did. Christine saw him go to the kitchen stove and burn the packet of papers. Turning to her, he explained that the group called "the tongues people" were just plain fanatical and were going crazy with this new doctrine. Thus, the pastor filled Christine's mind with prejudice against this "new" practice.

After Christine completed her week of meetings there, she returned to Faith Home in East Providence. She had not been in the house very long when Miss Emma Knowlton, a lady who also lived in Faith Home and with whom Miss Eckman had sweet fellowship, approached Christine with the subject of the outpouring of the Holy Spirit. She told Christine that apostolic days had returned and that people were receiving the Holy Ghost, speaking with other tongues as the Holy Spirit gave utterance, such as happened on the day of Pentecost. Before Christine could say anything, Emma thrust some papers into her hand, saying, "Read all about it. It is wonderful!" Christine then threw the papers on the table, just as if she had been stung by a viper. "Emma, do not accept all of that stuff! Brother N. says it is error and that the people are fanatical and crazy."

To this, Emma replied, "Oh, my child, do not be prejudiced! You are not acting like a sanctified person."

Christine turned away from her and went to her room. There God spoke to her from His Word, saying, (about the Bereans): "[They] were more noble than those in Thessalonica, in that they received the word with all readiness of mind, and searched the scriptures daily, whether those things were so" (Acts 17:11). Christine felt ashamed of herself and returned to the kitchen where Emma was working. She then asked Emma to give her one of the papers, promising, "I will prayerfully read its contents, and I believe that the Lord will protect me from error and will show me the truth of the matter."

The following day was Friday, and while Christine fasted and prayed, God guided her into truth. She was led to read the eleventh chapter of Deuteronomy.

That day God gave her light concerning the outpouring of the Holy Spirit as a type of the early and the latter rain. Verse 14 of this chapter was opened up to her, with these divisions: (1) the people — I will give you; (2) the gift — the rain of your land; (3) the time — in His due season; (4) the results — the first rain and the latter rain; and (5) the production of the rain — corn and wine and oil, a rich harvest, fruitfulness, and so forth. Upon comparing other passages of Scripture, Christine was convinced that the latter rain was falling, and that the saints were to ask for the rain in the time of the latter rain. (See Zechariah 10:1.)

As she continued to search the Scriptures, it was revealed to her that the early rain — a type of the outpoured Spirit — came at the beginning of the church's dispensation and had already been fulfilled. The outpouring of the early rain produced apostles, prophets, teachers, and pastors. From this outpouring, an outstanding work was done in the early church. Christine realized, however, that it was still the church age and God had promised that in the last days, He would pour out of His Spirit upon all flesh. (See Joel 2:28, 29.)

She was so touched by these truths that she sobbed before the Lord. She saw that the same sign which followed the early outpouring, giving assurance that "this was that spoken by the prophet Joel," would also accompany the latter outpouring. Yes, rain was falling again! Another shower had arrived. The refreshing from His presence had come. "For with stammering lips and another tongue will He speak to this people" (Isa. 28:11).

Christine knew that this Pentecostal sign was God's way of informing His people that the rest and the refreshing had come. O, how thrilled she was!

That very day Christine promised God that she would be true to the illumination He had given her on the Scriptures. She also promised that she would tarry until she was endued with power from on high. That evening she went to the little church and preached the message that God had given her. At first it "stirred up a hornet's nest." Some greatly opposed the teaching because of the Holiness doctrine of sanctification which was the second blessing, and they believed that there was nothing further to obtain. God held the little pastor steady and kept her heart in perfect peace. Thus, in due time, she and many other members of the church there received their portion of the latter rain of Pentecost, and spoke with other tongues as the Spirit gave utterance.

After introducing the Pentecostal truth to the little group of believers in the Holiness church where she was pastoring, she felt led to call a week of prayer meetings. The response was gratifying. Just a few members continued to oppose the Pentecostal truth which had been brought to them, and chose to refrain from attending the prayer meetings.

One of the strange and remarkable occurrences during those days was the receipt of a letter from Rev. Reuben A Gibson, her preacher friend, informing her that he had just returned from a missionary conference in Nyack, New York, conducted by the Christian and Missionary Alliance group with whom he was associated. In the letter he mentioned the mighty outpouring of the Spirit in Pentecostal fashion at the meetings, and that he had heard, for the first time, the speaking with other tongues as the Spirit gave utterance. He also wrote in his letter that God had given him this Pentecostal baptism and that he was praying for the saints in East Providence to receive a similar experience.

The letter was read to the church by Pastor Eckman, and the people asked her to invite him to speak at some of their meetings. Christine did this, and he came and spoke at a few evening prayer meetings. His preaching was very instructive and they were encouraged to "tarry until." Some fell under the power of God and received their portion. However, Christine did not receive the evidence of the baptism with the Holy Spirit during those meetings, although she was greatly revived in her spirit.

After a few weeks she received an invitation to visit the Rochester Bible Training School in Rochester, New York. [This was likely in the spring of 1910.] The school had been founded in 1906 by Elizabeth V. Baker and her sisters, Mary E. Work, Nellie A. Fell, Susan A. Duncan, and Harriet M. Duncan. Earlier, they had opened a mission and the Elim Faith Home there, in 1895. Christine had heard that they, too, had come into the light of the Pentecostal outpouring, and was very eager to meet them.

The night before she left East Providence, a tarrying meeting was held at the church. She sought earnestly for the baptism, hoping to receive it before she left for Rochester. She did not speak in tongues; however, God gave her a vision.

In this vision Christine saw a door open, and someone who looked like a heavenly being entered through the door. The words, *"Receive ye the Holy Ghost,"* were given to her. Holy laughter came upon Christine, and she was shaken by a mighty supernatural power. However, she did not speak in tongues during this manifestation and was somewhat disappointed.

The tarrying meeting closed, and on the way home, a sister of the church said to Christine, "Did you receive the Holy Ghost tonight?"

"Yes," Christine replied, "by faith, even though I have not as yet received the evidence of speaking in tongues." The lady thought that it was strange to hear Sister Eckman say this, because she had been teaching that unknown tongues would accompany the baptism of the Holy Ghost. Christine was a bit perplexed herself, but she did not intend to cast away her confidence in God. Before she retired that night, she thanked the Lord for the baptism of the Holy Spirit.

The next morning she packed her suitcase and prepared to travel from Providence to Rochester, New York, where she was to spend a short vacation. Before leaving the house, she sought the Lord in prayer, asking for a Scripture that would give her light and rest about the experience of the past evening. She was then impressed to read the fourth chapter of Romans, which was a favorite of hers. When she read verse 11, her spiritual eyes received an illumination from God. "And he received the sign of circumcision, a seal of the righteousness of the faith which he had, yet being uncircumcised." God showed her that He had called her to a life of faith, calling the things that be not as though they were. (See verse 17.) This was a faith similar to Abraham's faith. God assured her that she would not be disappointed. She had claimed the baptism with the Holy Ghost by faith, and the seal of that baptism would be given her in the sign evidence of "speaking with other tongues."

During the chapel service of the first night in Rochester, she was called upon to give a testimony. Christine arose, and testified that she had received the Holy Spirit by faith, but was waiting for the utterance of the Spirit for her to speak with other tongues. She immediately perceived that her testimony was not accepted by some, but when she sat down, her spirit witnessed that God approved of the words she had spoken. This brought peace to her soul, for there is "peace in believing."

The next morning the Duncan sisters called Christine to join them for a devotional hour. As they were kneeling in prayer, Christine was very conscious of the presence of the Lord. She felt that her faith was about to be rewarded, for her heart seemed to be bubbling over with joy. Mrs. Baker called on Christine to pray, and she began to pray in English, as usual. However, suddenly her language was changed and she was praying in a language that she did not understand. She knew, however, that this was indeed the sign evidence of her baptism, and she was filled with joy, shaking all over. God had indeed honored her faith and sealed her unto the Day of Redemption. *Hallelujah!*

Later that day, Mrs. Baker sent for Christine again and questioned, "What language did you speak in South America?"

Christine replied, "I was born in a British colony and received my education in an English school. Why do you ask?"

Mrs. Baker then said, "Well, you prayed so fluently in another language that I thought that it might be one you knew and spoke in South America."

"Sister Baker," Christine replied, "God has given me the sign of tongues as a seal of my baptism which I took by faith, and this morning was the first time I ever spoke in another language."

Christine remained in Rochester for several days, and had blessed fellowship with the leaders of that work. The results of her baptism with the Holy Spirit have been varied and far-reaching.

Chapter 11
When I Am Weak,
Then Am I Strong

"My grace is sufficient for thee; for my strength is made perfect in weakness"

(2 Cor. 12:9a).

Having told of Sister Christine Eckman's visit to the Elim Home and Bible School in Rochester — the home where the dear Lord sealed her with the Holy Spirit of promise — I would like to relate a very definite dealing of God in the revealing of His future plan for her life. Some of this plan had been shown to her in past visions, although she had not as yet fully understood certain portions of it.

As the train journeyed on, taking her to Rochester, she began to read her Bible. Her attention was called to a passage found in Romans 15:1-3. She re-read verse 3 — "For even Christ pleased not himself; but, as it is written, The reproaches of them that reproached thee fell on me." A vision was then given to her of Christ bearing the reproaches of others. He was bent beneath the load. She was attracted to the look on His face — so marred and so sad — and her heart went out to Him in intense sympathy. She knew that this was a Calvary scene and how she wished that she could have been there to bear some of the sufferings and to help change the situation for Him!

While these thoughts were surging through her mind, she was startled to see the face of Jesus slowly changing into the face and form of another. As she looked, she realized that instead of seeing Jesus, she was seeing her friend, Reuben A. Gibson. He seemed to be bowed down under a heavy load and his face was sorrowful. These words were then spoken to her inner being: *"Would you be willing to share his burdens and help to change his situation?"*

Before leaving for Rochester, Brother Gibson had called Christine and again broached the subject of marriage. At that time he told her that he had the mind of God in the matter, and that, if she would yield herself, she would also be shown that this union was of the Lord. He was indeed passing through a time of perplexity, and her heart was truly moved with pity for him.

To backtrack a bit further in their years of friendship, a number of years had passed since they first met, but the providence of God seemed to bring them together again and again. He became a frequent visitor at Faith Home where she resided. He also assisted her on several occasions at the mission church where she was pastoring. He resigned his church in Foxboro, Massachusetts, since he felt that God wanted him to live in East Providence. Church folks seemed pleased about his being at the mission church, since the Lord had really made his ministry a blessing to them. They had even asked Christine to have him fill the pulpit while she visited Rochester. This association made him feel sure that God was bringing them together in marriage. However, she was still not clear in her mind about the union. She did know, however, that she cared for him.

The morning she left for Rochester, Brother Gibson met her at the station, saying that he had come to let her know that he would never again bother her with his affairs. He asked her to please forget his offer of marriage. He looked so sad and despondent that her heart bled for him, but she did not leave him with any hope whatsoever that she would change her mind. She did tell him, however, that she was earnestly praying for God to solve his problems.

With this as a background, one can see what this vision meant to her that came as she was reading the fifteenth chapter of Romans on the train. At first she was frightened, but in a few moments, her spirit was quieted, and she was able to say, "God, help me to enter into Thy will for my life, and like Jesus, not to please myself, but to accept whatever you are pleased to lay upon me."

After a few minutes of meditation, she put out a fleece (typical of what Gideon did in the book of Judges): "Dear Lord, if this vision is of you, lead Brother Gibson to write a letter to me with a repeated proposal of marriage. Then I shall be sure that I am not being deceived by Satan." She knew that only God could make him do this, so she felt secure in putting out such a fleece.

She arrived safely in Rochester and soon became lost in her new-found joy of receiving the baptism with the Holy Spirit. A few days before she left the Elim Home to return to East Providence, the answer to her fleece came. A letter arrived from Brother Gibson. The following is a portion of its contents: "I presume that you will be disgusted with my weakness, but I cannot help doing this. The urge to write to you is so strong upon me that I am making one more attempt to ask you to reconsider your refusal to marry me, and to send me a favorable answer. I shall be praying to that end."

As she read the letter, she realized that God had answered her fleece. She knew that she was being called of God into this union with Brother Gibson. She sent him a brief note in answer to his letter. It read, "Your letter received. Leaving Rochester on . . . Meet me at the train. Will give you my answer when I see you."

The train pulled into East Providence where Reuben was waiting anxiously for Christine's return. After exchanging greetings, he asked, "Have you brought me a favorable answer?"

She smiled and then said, "Let us go into the station and talk things over." As they sat there together, she told him of her experience on the train and of the fleece she had put out, describing how God had answered her request. Then she said, "I am ready to fall in line with God's plans for our lives."

Needless to say, Reuben was greatly relieved, for he had come to the train station in fear and trembling. The two of them sat in the station for some time, feeling that God's presence was with them, and they were both very happy.

The days which followed her decision to marry Brother Gibson, however, were days filled with perplexity. They both needed divine wisdom to guide them, and stood upon the Scripture, "If any of you lack wisdom, let him ask of God who giveth to all men liberally, and upbraideth not, and it shall be given him. But let him ask in faith, nothing wavering" (James 1:5,6).

Repeatedly, they asked God in prayer for wisdom in arranging their future.

The church that Sister Christine pastored had to be informed of the step she was taking, and of course, she didn't know what their attitudes would be. However, God undertook and she met with very little opposition. Brother Gibson's successful ministry among them during her absence in Rochester, New York, gave the majority of the members confidence that the combined ministries of Reuben and Christine would greatly bless the church.

Her most severe test came from the folks with whom she lived, Brother and Sister Crocker, managers of Faith Home. They refused to believe that she was being led of the Lord, and Brother Crocker was so terribly opposed to the marriage that the fellowship between Brother Gibson and him was absolutely severed. Truly, if Christine had not known so definitely the mind of God concerning the marriage, Brother Crocker could likely have succeeded in making her waver. The Lord surely sustained her during those days as she sought Him in fervent prayer.

Many of her friends warned her that she was running a risk to enter a home and take on the responsibility of motherless children who were not her own. Even her own dear sister who stood so loyally with her throughout their lives, felt a little fearful about this step that she was about to take. God's ways, however, are not easily understood by human minds and many times in our obedience to His call, we are misunderstood by those who love us. Christine assured Alice that God had called her to stand with Brother Gibson, even though she felt that there would be problems to face. She told her that God's will was her delight, and that she knew He would take her through every difficult situation.

The weeks went by, and soon it was time for the wedding. Brother Gibson's home was small and not really suitable for the family, so he rented a house on Anthony Street, several blocks from the Faith Home where Christine was living.

When he had first come to live in East Providence, he and his children were entirely cast upon God for the supply of their needs. Later, however, after some very severe testing, he felt led to apply for a position as floor walker at the Boston Store in Providence. Thus, at the time of their marriage, he was occupied in secular work. Christine did not believe that this was God's best for them since both of them understood the life of faith, looking wholly to God for the supplying of their needs throughout their years of Christian service. It seemed, however, the thing that had to be done for the time being, so she kept silent and waited for the Lord to bring about the change. Brother Gibson desired to make her happy and beautifully furnished their new home.

The wedding was a rather quiet affair. The ceremony and reception took place in Mrs. George Carpenter's home on Taunton Avenue in East Providence on November 10, 1910. Sister Carpenter was the secretary of their church at that time, and she and her good husband furnished the reception supper as their gift to them. Just a few of their intimate friends were invited to the wedding. Another dear sister who was a close friend of the couple invited them to her lovely home located some miles out of Providence, and there they were royally entertained for the first two weeks of their marriage. Those days were long remembered because of blessings received as they waited upon their God in prayer for a fresh anointing of the Holy Spirit to fit them for future ministry together.

I know not what awaits me, God kindly veils mine eyes,
And o'er each step of my onward ways He makes new scenes
    to rise.
In every joy He sends me comes a sweet and glad surprise,
    One step I see before me, is all I need to see.
    The light of heaven more brightly shines
        When earth's illusions flee.
        Sweetly through the silence
        Came His loving: "Follow Me."
O blissful lack of wisdom, 'tis blessed not to know —
He holds me with His own right hand and will not let me go.
He lulls my troubled soul to rest, in Him Who loves me so,
    So on I go, not knowing, I would not if I might;

When I Am Weak, Then Am I Strong

> I'd rather walk in the dark with God
> than go alone in the light;
> I'd rather walk with faith in Him, than go alone by sight.
> Where He may lead, I'll follow, my trust in Him repose,
> And every hour in perfect peace, I'll sing, "He knows, He knows."
> (Mary G. Braynard)

Christine moved from Faith Home to join her husband and children. They continued as pastors of the little church on Ivy Street until, after a strange series of events, Sister Gibson felt constrained of the Lord to leave her husband's home and to return to Faith Home. On that day, in the early years of this century, a solitary figure could be seen walking south on Broadway in East Providence.

When Christine and Reuben were married, Christine took on the responsibilities of a wife and became a mother to four motherless children. (The oldest child had left home by that time.) It was rather difficult at first to adjust to housekeeping in her new surroundings, but with the help of her dear sister Alice (who had come to live with them), things worked out very nicely in the months that followed. The dear Lord gave Christine one year of happiness as a new bride. Trials then began in a variety of ways. I will mention one of these in this chapter.

Christine was suddenly stricken with an attack of appendicitis. Her husband was working as floor manager in the local Boston Store, and when he came home that evening, he was so very tired that he did not seem to realize that Christine's case was serious. The next day while Christine was in deep agony, God sent one of her dearest friends to her. (She was the one who had opened her lovely home to them at the time of their wedding.) Upon seeing Christine's condition, she called for her personal physician to examine her. He quickly ordered her to be taken to the Rhode Island Hospital.

Brother Gibson was called home and when he saw her critical condition, he consented to an operation which they prepared for immediately. Her case was indeed serious and even when the doctors gave little hope that she would recover, God undertook and she was miraculously healed. Afterward she found out that a group of four saintly women had spent an entire night in intercessory prayer for her recovery, receiving the assurance that she would be healed. Thank God for that answer to prayer! After her recovery, a friend in Newport, Rhode Island, took her, with Reuben's consent, to her home and had a nurse care for her until she was well again.

At that time [c. 1911], there was a Pentecostal Campmeeting in session at Mount Waite in Massachusetts. Her friend thought that it might do Christine good to spend a few days at the campground, so she rented a cottage. Alice accompanied Christine to the camp.

It was there that she met her "Waterloo" — her first great battle of her married life. However, God had prepared her for this experience a few days before she went to the camp by giving her a sermon from the book of Obadiah. In verse 21 it reads, "And saviors shall come up on Mount Zion to judge the mount of Esau." Christine thought that possibly she would have an opportunity to give the message while at the camp, but the opportunity never came. The message was given to her to prepare her for her own crucifixion.

Among the ministers at the camp was one with whom she had become acquainted a few months before her marriage. He had heard about Brother Gibson and had tried to persuade her not to marry him. He did not know, however, of God's definite dealing with her — he only knew that she was now married to the man against whom he was so prejudiced.

One afternoon the meeting was opened for testimonies, and Christine felt the urge of the Holy Spirit to rise and testify of the goodness of God in her life. She had just begun to speak when this minister who was sitting with others on the platform, rose and harshly commanded her to sit down. Before she could do so, he began to tell the audience a most unbelievable story about Brother Gibson, also relating how he had warned her not to marry Reuben. He continued by calling her several abominable names. At first she was so stunned that she thought she would faint and fall to the ground. However, suddenly, she felt the presence of Jesus. She seemed to feel His arms around her and these words were whispered into her ears, *"My child, be of good cheer. You are a partaker of my sufferings. I died in the open. The people sat and watched me there on the cross. Saviors are made only through death and resurrection."*

These words from the lips of her Savior brought new life into her body and calmed her nerves. Her spirit was lifted into the heavenlies, and joy was poured into her soul instead of sorrow. When she came to herself, the meeting was over and the people were leaving the crude wooden tabernacle. Her dear sister looked greatly distressed as she said to her, "Christine, let's get out of here. This is awful!"

Before she could reply, Christine found herself clasped in the arms of a well-dressed lady, who said to her, "He will suffer for this. I am disgusted with him for doing this to you." The lady went on to explain that she was the wife of the man who had verbally attacked her.

Sister Gibson assured her that God had permitted it and that she was not disturbed over what her husband had done. This lady was the only person who had the courage to come and talk with her about the outburst. Every other person "passed by on the other side," Christine later remarked.

It was dinner time and her sister said, "Christine, surely you are not going into that dining hall, are you?"

"I paid for our meals, and feel perfectly calm now, and also rather hungry. Please come along and let us eat," Christine replied.

They entered the dining hall and Christine could feel all eyes upon her. However, she was not perturbed, for her beloved Jesus had assured her that He was with her. She knew that God's grace is sufficient and that His strength is made perfect in weakness. Therefore, she sat in the dining hall and "took pleasure in the reproach." Had she not promised the Lord that she would let the reproach of another fall on her? Then should she shrink from this trial that she had just passed through? "Oh no!" Christine exclaimed in her heart. Most gladly would she rather glory in reproaches that the power of Christ may rest upon her.

> The cross that He gave may be heavy,
> But it ne'er outweighs His grace;
> The storm that I feared may surround me,
> But it ne'er excludes His face.
> His will I have joy in fulfilling
> As I'm walking in His sight;
> My all to the blood I am bringing,
> It alone can keep me right.
>
> The Cross is not greater than His grace;
> The storm cannot hide His blessed face;
> I am satisfied to know
> That with Jesus here below,
> I can conquer every foe.
>
> (Commander Ballington Booth)

Chapter 12
Have the Faith of God

"Not by might, nor by power, but by my Spirit, saith the Lord of hosts."

(Zech. 4:6c).

The reasons for Sister Gibson leaving her home heartbroken after one year of marriage were perhaps two-fold — one being the fact that her husband, a man with great oratorical abilities and deep understanding and knowledge of the Scriptures, had remained in his position at the Boston Store in Providence. Each morning he would rise, dress, put a white flower in his lapel and go off to work. Sister Gibson knew that this was not God's will for his life, for, before being joined together in marriage, he had promised that he would work with her in the ministry, and that together they would pastor the church, which, by now, had been reduced to eleven members because of death or removal. However, he did not keep his promise. He would be very tired at times, slipping into a meeting and falling asleep time and time again. Of course, this was quite disturbing to Christine.

Another reason was that the home where the Gibsons lived was being used for activities that Sister Gibson felt did not please the Lord in any way. The children did not seem to lean toward the things of God, and worldliness had crept in.

She made these reasons known to her husband one morning as he was preparing for work. She said, "Papa, when you come home this evening, I will not be here. As long as you labor in that store and allow this house to be used for purposes which do not glorify the name of the Lord, I do not feel that I can remain with you."

Reuben laughed and said, "Christine, you don't mean that."

"Yes, I do, Papa," Christine replied.

"If you do that, I want you to know that we are through, one with the other," Reuben retorted.

Reuben went off to work feeling very confident that Christine would be in her place when he arrived home, but, as you have already read, the solitary figure made her way back to Faith Home that very day.

Christine knew that she had to be willing to be misjudged and misunderstood, by both friends and foes. The first few days after she arrived back at Faith Home were very trying ones for her. No one seemed to understand what her returning was all about. She could hear some of the elderly folk in the home talking her affairs over with each other. Two very deaf women yelled out, "Why did she leave her husband? Did he put her out of the house?" And so it went for days.

Then, her own dear sister Alice, who could not understand why, was watching every move that Christine made. Sister Gibson had asked her to stay in the home and to look after Reuben and the children, making their meals and so forth, but Alice replied, "I am going with you. You need someone to watch over you. You seem to be losing your mind." She thought that Christine was making a terrible mistake in leaving her husband and her home, but God opened Alice's eyes to the situation.

Sister Gibson was very friendly with dear Sister Emma Knowlton who was a great woman of prayer. Together they prayed things through many times. Emma Knowlton's words of encouragement enlightened many of Christine's very dark hours.

The two kind retired missionaries, Brother and Sister Thomas Crocker, were still managing Faith Home and were doing what they could for elderly homeless people who sought refuge under their roof. Unable to make ends meet, the Crockers had hung a "For Sale" sign on the house.

Soon after Sister Gibson came to stay in the home, she rose up in the power of the Spirit and was commanded by God to compass the grounds seven times. As she began to do so, a few elderly ladies stood at their windows wagging their heads, believing that something was wrong. What they saw was a woman wading about in tall grass, compassing the grounds, not once, but seven times. Surely she is not well, they thought, but as far as Sister Gibson was concerned, she was claiming the ground for Zion.

When she returned to the home, the Spirit told her that it was God's sign, and as she had done, so also would He do. The land would not be sold. He also spoke to her through the beautiful 48th Psalm which has since become the beloved Psalm of all Zionians. In her obedience, she had preserved the home for God's purposes.

Later that evening, after prayer, God revealed to her that she and Brother Gibson would be reconciled and that together they would become the future managers of Faith Home. This was also revealed to her sister Alice, and the latter came and told her what the Lord had shown to her as Christine was walking around the grounds. This, indeed, brought much joy to Sister Gibson's heart. It was the turning point, and God began to work mightily. Sister Gibson was assured that she had truly been given a sign. As Mary of old, Christine kept all these things in her heart and pondered upon them, placing her trust and confidence in God, who doeth all things well.

The days that followed the manifestation of the Holy Spirit, when she was led to walk around the grounds and compass the property, were truly days of communion with God. She had the assurance that He had brought her to Faith Home to save it for His future purposes. No matter what God's purposes might be, she was sure that the property would never be sold into the hands of the ungodly.

Two weeks passed, and on the following Sunday morning, as she was preparing for church, God revealed to her that something strange was going to happen in the service that day. As she stood up in the chapel to deliver the sermon which God had given her the previous evening, the door opened and her husband walked in. He looked as though he had been ill; his eyes were sunken, suggesting the shedding of many tears.

For a moment, the sight of him disturbed Christine, but soon the Spirit calmed her. As Reuben took his seat in the congregation, she gave her text and preached what God had given her. At the close of the message, Reuben rose with tears streaming down his cheeks and came to the platform. He turned to Christine and said, "Wife, I have failed you — please forgive me." Then, to the congregation he said, "I have failed my God and you. I am here to ask forgiveness and to solicit your prayers."

O, what a day that was! The entire church wept. They all fell upon their knees and united in a prayer which ascended to the throne of grace on behalf of Brother Gibson. After the service, Brother and Sister Gibson walked from the church to Faith Home which was located a few blocks from the church building. As they walked, he related to her the dream that had changed his feelings toward her and had brought him to true repentance before God.

In the dream, Reuben was aware that Sister Gibson had left him, but some of her clothes were still in his home. His daughter, Hattie, reminded him that Christine needed the clothes and that he should take them to her. He and his daughter came to visit Christine where she was living, and they brought a package of clothing for her. It was dinner time, and they were invited to stay for dinner. At the table sat a man with his head resting in his hands. At first Brother Gibson could not see his face. He realized that this man was her new husband and that she was lost to Reuben. Turning to his daughter, Reuben said, "Hattie, mother will not return to us. She is married to another."

Just as he said this, he heard Sister Gibson's voice saying, "Reuben, let me introduce you to my husband." The man looked up, and Brother Gibson realized that he was looking into the face of Jesus. The hands of Jesus were raised, as if to bless the food, and Reuben saw the nail-pierced hands of his Savior.

This dream affected Reuben deeply. He told Christine that he awoke sobbing and went down on his knees by the bed. God then spoke to him, and Reuben knew that he would have to return to the Pentecostal Holiness church, see his wife and ask forgiveness. He obeyed the voice of God that day.

The couple parted at the Faith Home entrance since Brother Gibson did not wish to meet the Crockers just then, but promised to do so later. Brother Crocker was very much upset when he heard that Christine and her husband had been reconciled, and he told his wife that he would have nothing more to do with the Gibsons.

The next morning was Monday and Sister Gibson went to the Crockers' apartment to pay her board which was taken care of weekly by the church. As she handed the money to Brother Crocker, he returned it to her with these angry words, "I refuse to take your unclean money!"

Christine was stunned at first and then realized that he thought the money had been given to her by Reuben. She asked him to explain his attitude toward her, and his answer made her understand that she was no longer wanted at Faith Home. She asked him to grant her a little time to seek the face of God as to what decision should be made. She went to her room and fell on her face.

God spoke to her, *"Go and tell Mr. Crocker to have your trunk placed on the sidewalk. Inform him that you will then follow the trunk by leaving Faith Home."*

She obeyed God and when Mr. Crocker heard what the Lord had said, he replied, "I will never do that."

Sister Crocker then began to weep and said, "Thomas, don't you dare hurt this woman! She is God's anointed, and we shall suffer if we turn her out of the house."

> **"They who trust in the Lord shall be as Mount Zion which cannot be removed, but abideth forever"**
> **(Ps. 125:1).**

The days that followed Sister Gibson's obedience to God were truly days of trust in the Lord — days of refusing to be removed from the stand which she had taken. She knew that it was a crisis moment when everything depended upon her loyalty to God.

O, how the enemy had tried to tempt her by human suggestions! One was to try and persuade her sister Alice, to return to Brother Gibson's home and help the children with the housekeeping. This really would have spoiled the plan of God for Zion. God, in His wisdom and love, overthrew this device of Satan. Alice was stricken ill and did not recover until Brother Gibson fell in line with God's will for him. Reuben then decided to give up his home and to make other accommodations for his children.

During those days, Mr. Crocker acted very strangely toward Christine. One morning, however, during a devotional period, the Holy Spirit gave her a ministry for him which completely changed his attitude. After prayers were finished, he asked Christine to see him in their apartment. As she entered, he stood before her, trembling and very ill. He then told her that God was dealing with him about his feelings toward Brother Gibson. He said that when she had the ministry for him that morning, scales fell from his eyes and he saw clearly that her vision of the Faith Home property was of God. He now realized that it should not be sold. He asked her to get in touch with Brother Gibson since he wanted him to come over as soon as possible to have a talk with him.

Later that day Brother Crocker became very ill and had to be put to bed. Sister Gibson quickly got in touch with her husband, and he came to Faith Home that night. He and Brother Crocker were closeted together for quite some time and then they called for Christine to come and pray for Brother Crocker's recovery. God, however, had revealed to Sister Gibson that Brother Crocker would die, so she could not pray a prayer of faith for his recovery.

Brother Gibson was so pleased that a reconciliation had taken place between them, that, of course, he desired Brother Crocker to go on living so that they could work together as in days past. However, God willed it otherwise. When Brother and Sister Gibson left the room, Christine told her husband that God had shown her that He was going to take Brother Crocker Home. Reuben was surprised and felt very sad about it, and about a week from that time, Brother Crocker died.

The Lord, nevertheless, kept Thomas Crocker alive until certain things were accomplished. One was the holding of the annual business meeting of the Faith Home Corporation. The directors met with Brother and Sister Crocker who were still the managers. Brother Crocker expressed his desire to have Brother and Sister Gibson on the board. He told them that God had shown him that Brother Gibson would fill his place. He also related Sister Gibson's vision regarding the saving of the property — a continuation of the work of faith in East Providence.

The majority of the directors agreed with Brother Crocker's desires and were willing to have a new board of directors formed. However, there was one man on the board who was bitterly opposed to this. He made it known by stamping his foot and saying, "I will oppose the Gibsons coming on this board as managers, as long as there is breath in my body!"

The opposition greatly perturbed Brother Crocker and added to his illness. Mrs. Crocker was also very much upset.

While the business meeting was being held downstairs, Sister Gibson was upstairs praying. During this time of prayer, God gave her a vision of the opposing board member. She saw him sitting on a round piano stool. Suddenly, he and the stool became a great mountain. These words then came to Sister Gibson, "Who art thou, O great mountain? Before Zerubbabel thou shalt become a plain: and he shall bring forth the headstone of it with shoutings, crying, Grace, grace unto it" (Zech. 4:7). The gift of faith seemed to take possession of Sister Gibson, and seeing the vision, she exclaimed, "Get out of God's way, you great mountain, and don't you dare hinder His plan!" In her vision she saw the man fall from the piano stool.

Christine was then reminded of the words of Jesus to His disciples, "Have the faith of God" (Mark 11:22).

Have the Faith of God 77

"For verily I say unto you, Whosoever shall say unto this mountain, Be thou removed, and be thou cast into the sea; and shall not doubt in his heart, but shall believe that those things which he saith shall come to pass; he shall have whatsoever he saith"
(Mark 11:23).

After the business meeting, a lady from the church came to Sister Gibson's room, along with Sister Crocker, who told Sister Gibson what had transpired during the meeting. The lady from the church suggested that they kneel and "pray this thing through." They knelt, and soon Christine rose from her knees and declared to the two women that the thing was done — they did not need to pray any longer. She was assured that the opposing board member would never be allowed to hinder the plan of God.

She asked Sister Crocker where this man was sitting in the business meeting, and Sister Crocker told Christine that he was sitting on a piano stool. God's visions are never off-course.

The vote of the board was sufficient to install the Gibsons as the new managers, in spite of the opposition of the one board member. This man died shortly thereafter.

God's way is the best way, my path He hath planned,
I'll trust in Him always while holding His hand.
In shadow or sunshine, He ever is near,
With Him for my refuge, I never need fear.
God's way shall be my way, He knoweth the best.
And leaning upon Him, sweet, sweet is my rest.
No harm shall befall me, safe, safe shall I be;
I'll cling to Him ever, so precious is He.
God's way is the best way,
God's way is the right way,
I'll trust in Him always,
He knoweth the best.
(Lida S. Leech)

Chapter 13
Though It Tarry, Wait for It

"Arise...go with them, doubting nothing; for I have sent them"

(Acts 10:20b).

The Church of the First Born gradually added to its membership, and by 1913, the following members were listed: Ruth A. Cleveland, Delia Richmond, Christine Gibson, Reuben A. Gibson, Alice S. Carpenter, Alice Dunn, Emma Knowlton, Anna King, Alice Gray, Jennie Sutherland, Matilda Jameson, Frank Koerner, Christine Koerner, Brother Lennox, Elizabeth Lennox, Carrie Gray, Elizabeth Olney, Earl Franklin and Emma Franklin.

As time went on, this congregation built a little chapel adjacent to Faith Home. It was not fully completed, yet was already too small to accommodate the crowds that attended the May and September conventions held there. A tent was being used for services while the basement of the chapel was used for meals. At this time, Sister Gibson had another remarkable vision.

While sitting at a noon meal, Sister Gibson saw a vision of a large tabernacle erected next to the chapel on the grounds which held, at that time, a potato patch. She was very quick to sense and follow the leading of the Lord and she immediately spoke to her husband and the assembled ministers concerning this vision. Her husband remarked, "She is such a visionary!" The others were not too receptive because, at the time, the little chapel was more than adequate for the needs of the regular services of the small congregation. The ministers expressed their objections in the kindest words possible, feeling that perhaps she was being a little too "visionary." However, she persisted in faith, without forcing her will or her ways upon her husband or the others, and simply began to trust God for the fulfillment of her vision.

God brought comfort and encouragement to Sister Gibson through the words of Habakkuk 2:3, "For the vision is yet for an appointed time, but at the end it shall speak, and not lie; though it tarry, wait for it, because it will surely come, it will not tarry."

He also gave her Psalm 48:2, "Beautiful for situation, the joy of the whole earth, is Mount Zion." The voice of God spoke to Christine's heart, telling her that this Scripture was for the establishment of a Bible school called Zion.

Shortly thereafter, the Gibsons were called to go to a humble mission in New York City to preach a campaign. Before they left for New York, Sister Gibson spoke once again to her husband concerning the vision. "Reuben, if the Lord were to give us $1,000.00 toward the new tabernacle while we are in New York, could I begin the building when we return?"

Brother Gibson's first reaction was to break into uproarious laughter. He then said, "If we get enough money from those people, dearie, to cover the expenses of our trip, we will be most fortunate. But if you get $1,000.00 on this trip, yes, you can come back and build your tabernacle."

The plans for the trip were completed and they journeyed to New York. The mission was, indeed, very humble; the people were extremely poor; and the place they were given for accommodations was quite inadequate. But these humble pioneers of faith accepted it without complaint. This was an opportunity to preach God's Word, to share His blessings with others, and everything else was incidental.

The meetings had not been in progress many days when Miss Mina Cartwright, a well-to-do Christian friend of the Gibsons, joined them for a service. She had heard that they were in town. After the service was over, she inquired, "But where are you staying? What? There? You can't stay in that place! You must come with me and stay in my home while you are here."

Their protestations did not avail, and since the leaders of the mission had no objection (and were perhaps relieved at having the burden of providing for them lifted), the Gibsons accepted her invitation.

A few mornings later, Sister Gibson and Sister Cartwright were doing breakfast dishes together and were in general conversation. (No mention was made of the revelation that had been given to Sister Gibson by the Holy Spirit.) Brother Gibson came into the kitchen and noticed the two ladies were quite engrossed in a discussion. He remarked, "I suppose my wife has been telling you all about her latest vision."

"Why, no," remarked Sister Cartwright, turning to Sister Gibson and inquiring, "Has the Lord given you a vision, dear? You must tell me all about it."

Sister Gibson then gave an account of how the vision had come to her and of the burden she felt because of it. As she finished, Sister Cartwright exclaimed, "You know, I feel it is of the Lord, and I want to give the first $1,000.00 toward the building!" What a rejoicing welled up in Sister Gibson's heart, and in the heart of her husband, too, for he had finally realized that God was in it and no one could gainsay its speaking. They shook each other's hand and the Gibsons soon returned to East Providence. With the $1,000.00, they began to build the large tabernacle that eventually came to be known as Sinclair Hall, the largest of the men's dormitories.

In those days, $1,000.00 was a lot of money, but it was only enough to barely begin to build a large, two-story building that was set to be 50 x 80, having a church on the second floor and dormitory rooms on the first, plus a fully finished cellar to contain kitchen and dining room facilities. The work began but soon came to a halt because of depleted funds.

It was at this time that Brother Dean Blanchard and his wife, Luna, came to Zion for a convention, saw the unfinished building, and were moved by the Lord to return to Vermont to sell their large dairy farm. They were to give all of their savings, plus the profit from the sale of the property, into the work of God. The Lord led them to cast their lot with the Zion family in Faith Home.

They, their children, along with Byron Hodgeman, came to East Providence. The money was devoted to finishing the tabernacle while Brother Blanchard and young Byron labored as carpenters on the building. It is a credit to their love, devotion, sacrifice, and expertise that, during a recent renovation of the building, both building inspectors and consulting contractors praised the soundness of the structure and noted that very special care was taken when the building was erected.

This would be a good time to tell of the manner in which the Blanchards, and later on, the Chases, became affiliated with Zion.

One winter's day as Sister Gibson was opening her mail, she noticed a letter with a Vermont postmark and return address of people by the name of Jelley, of whom she had never heard.

(Unbeknownst to her at that time, the Jelley family would one day become a part of Zion's family, helping in many ways to further the work of faith.) She opened the letter, and as she read, she learned that these people had read a Pentecostal periodical, *Word and Work,* telling of marvelous outpourings of the Holy Spirit upon groups of people all over the world. They learned that folks were receiving manifestations of fulfillment, with the speaking of unknown tongues. Some folks in Vermont had already received their baptism this way; however, they did not fully understand it.

They noticed Christine Gibson's name and address in this magazine. Therefore, they wrote to her, asking that she come to Vermont to give them teaching on this subject.

Just as she finished and folded the letter, her husband came into the room and she then related its contents to him. He remarked, "You cannot go up there, dear. This is the middle of the winter. I cannot go with you, because I have to be here to supervise the building of the chapel [which, at that time, had not yet been finished]. No, I think you had better refuse that invitation."

He left the room, and after a little while, Sister Gibson picked up the letter and prayed over it. God quickened to Christine's heart the words that the Spirit spoke to Peter on the rooftop when he was to be sent to the home of the Roman centurion. Peter had received a vision of a sheet let down from heaven and he saw unclean things in it. He was commanded to rise, kill and eat, but he disobeyed because he didn't want to eat anything unclean. God reprimanded him, saying, "What God hath cleansed, that call not thou common" (Acts 10:15b). This Scripture came to Sister Gibson the same way that it had come to Peter. God said, "Arise, therefore, and get thee down, and go with them, doubting nothing" (Acts 10:20a).

When Brother Gibson returned to the room, she told him of her experience. He, knowing how she responded so quickly to anointed words, said, "Alright, call up your friend, Miss Prudence in Boston, and if she can go with you on the train and be with you, I will give my consent."

The two ladies boarded the train one day to make the trip to Windsor, Vermont. Sister Gibson wondered how she would identify the people who had invited her to come. As soon as she stepped from the train, she saw a small child standing nearby, wearing a sandwich sign. One side read, "Jesus is coming soon," and the other was something similar. She knew right away that this was one of the party to whom she should introduce herself. The Jelleys told her that the meetings were to begin on Monday night in a certain place which they had hired.

The next day was Sunday and Sister Gibson and Miss Prudence decided to attend the leading church in Windsor, which was a Baptist church pastored by a Rev. Waldron. Sister Gibson was enjoying the message when she suddenly felt led to rise and extend an invitation to the group, to attend the series of meetings that she was going to begin the next evening.

Sister Gibson was not a forward woman; she was not a rude woman; but she was a woman who yielded quickly and promptly to the urgings of the Spirit. She prayed, "Lord, if the pastor stops a noticeable length of time until it seems as though he can't go on, I will rise and invite him and his congregation to our meetings."

In a few minutes she noticed that the church grew quiet and the pastor was just standing there, saying nothing. Christine quickly jumped up, identified herself, and invited the people to the meetings. Of course many people in the church thought, "What a rude woman!" and "To think that we would go to those meetings!" One of the people who thought that this was a very rude action on the part of Sister Gibson was the young lady who was the church organist. Her name was Alice Chase. Her father was the head deacon in the church, and her brothers and sister attended this church also. Later Christine found out that Alice greatly resented the interruption in the service.

After Christine finished her invitation, the pastor completed his sermon, dismissed the service, and went back to the door to greet the people. As Christine and Miss Prudence came near, he remarked, "I know what that was all about — I have a Pentecostal mother!"

Monday evening's meeting was very well attended and each night, more people came. There was a wonderful revival led by the Holy Spirit. The organist, Alice Chase, her father, her brothers, Newton and Henry, her stepmother, Ellen Chase, Byron Hodgeman, Brother and Sister Blanchard, and several others received the Pentecostal experience. Sister Gibson remained there quite a while. The meetings were so blessed of God that revival fires kept on burning.

One day, who should appear, but Reuben! He had come to take his wife home. However, they constrained him to give some teaching before they left, and he ministered the Word to them in his own special way.

Reuben and Pastor Waldron of the Baptist church became very good friends. Later, Brother Gibson invited him to a convention in East Providence. He came, and during that time, he, too, received the wonderful experience of the infilling of the Holy Spirit with the evidence of speaking in tongues. He went through a great deal of persecution for the stand that he took, but God blessed him and made him a blessing.

Thus, in this way, Sister Gibson met some of the very early workers and friends whose names are often heard in connection with the work at Zion.

Chapter 14
The Exercise of Faith

> "Who through faith...wrought righteousness, obtained promises...out of weakness were made strong, waxed valiant in fight"
>
> (Heb. 11:33, 34).

In June of 1915, Reuben and Christine began a "Journal Devoted to the Life of Faith and Present Truth." They named it, *Faith*.

Volume I, Number 1 was printed with the following inscription on its cover:

> *This Journal contains a record of the period from June 1, 1913 to June 1, 1915, including also an outline of the past history of the Home, and its work under its present management, as a testimony of God's faithfulness in hearing and answering prayer.*

A further explanatory note reports that it is the first published report of Faith Home founded by the late Alpheus A. Cleveland and afterwards for a period of ten years, cared for under the management of the late Thomas C. Crocker.

Excerpts from Reuben's article, *A Work of Faith*, follow:

> Two years ago in the providence of God, the management of Faith Home was transferred to myself and wife. The Home was founded by the late Alpheus A. Cleveland and later, for a period of ten years, was under the care and management of the late Thomas

C. Crocker who fell asleep in Jesus on June 1, 1913. Thus, it will be seen that it is just two years since we entered our life of trust in connection with the Home. We now believe it to be the will of God to send forth a statement recording God's faithfulness to us in caring for us, and supplying the needs of the Home in the bountiful way which it has pleased Him to do during that time.

Perhaps it will be well to state here, that through the grace of God, I had, previous to my coming to the Home, been enabled of Him to trust Him wholly for many years, for all my needs, in missionary labors in British Guiana, South America, and in the West Indies [Barbados], my native home. I looked to Him in the intervening years of my missionary labors and in my coming to the Home. This was accomplished during a process of trial and suffering which was used of God to lead me into a deeper knowledge of His will and a clearer understanding of His ways. With a praiseful heart I thank Him for all the ways it has pleased Him to lead me, for the way He is still leading, and for what I have learned in His school of faith and obedience.

Looking back over those earlier years of His training, I see so much of fleshly glory, the love of human praise, and the earthliness of human vision. I marvel at the forbearance, kindness, and love of God in accepting and blessing the efforts and labors of those days. I am comforted, however, in seeing those experiences as a part of His training and teachings, in preparing His chosen, but unworthy vessel, for all He has called us for, and is leading us to.

"He led them forth by the right way"
(Ps. 107:7).

The right way is not always the easy, nor the short, way. It is not always the way we would choose, nor the way our friends and observers would have us go. God's way is always the right way, though we may not see it to be so at the time, nor understood to be so by others.

"Thy way is in the sea and thy path in the great waters, and thy footsteps are not known"
(Ps. 77:19).

And so it comes to pass that when God has a new program for our lives, we are sure to be criticized by those who cannot see nor understand the way He is leading us. That way is oftentimes shrouded with mystery and obscurity, so that the natural eyes, even of those He is leading, cannot and do not see the way through. Is it not so, then, that His program for our lives, being much larger than our plans, and reaching much farther than any human vision, can only be perfected in a life of faith, one step at a time? It calls for a perfect yieldedness and submission to His will that is only ours by the crucifixion of our plans and the sacrifice of our all.

Through such leadings of God, I, like Abram, "Went up out of Egypt...unto the place where his tent had been at the beginning...unto the place of the altar, which he had made there at the first: and there Abram called on the name of the Lord." (See Genesis 13:1,3 and 4.)

There are no finalties with God in His calling of us, and leading us forth to a life of faith; there are stages and processes, but each stage and process is a link in the chain of God's plan and purpose in every true life of faith.

So, on May 31, 1913, releasing myself from a salaried position, parting with such worldly goods as myself and family had, and making a burnt offering consecration of ourselves to God, we cast ourselves on Him to trust Him for all things, to serve Him in His glorious Gospel as He should enable us, going forth hereafter, as pilgrims and strangers to wait for His Son from heaven.

The passing away of Brother Crocker the day after my leaving a salaried position and giving up what earthly home comforts I had, came both as a surprise and a witness that I had not mistaken the will of God in taking the step I had, to follow Him in a complete life of trust which I am sure He had called me to, and had been dealing with me to bring me into.

There were certain conditions in the home which we quickly saw would have to undergo some changes in order for it to be brought into the plan which God had shown us. There were twenty persons living in Faith Home. Seven or eight of these were giving small amounts toward their living expenses. We knew that this was not what God wanted. The purpose and aim of the home was for each occupant to live a life of believing prayer, cast wholly on Him for the supply of every need. The presence of these parties in the home hindered such a testimony. They were not in the home primarily to reap spiritual benefits — they were there because it was an affordable lodging place.

We were careful in making the change so as not to inconvenience the residents. We notified each one that the home was chartered for homeless, evangelical Christians, and that, under our management, it would be open to those seeking rest, spiritual help, physical healing, and the Baptism with the Holy Ghost with signs following. We stated that it, having no endowment fund, would be henceforth supported by voluntary contributions that had been received in answer to prayer, through faith in God. It was our intent that the occupants of the home would either be those united with us by their faith and prayers for the support and work of the home, or be there for one or more of the reasons listed above.

It seemed to be God's thought for us to make those changes slowly and gradually, and we found in doing so, both the parties who went out, and the home were each better served and satisfied. That change being effected, we were now without any visible means of support whatever, and the home was free to carry out those purposes and principles which God had shown us. Those permanently residing in the home and those coming to us were now to be united in purpose for the following:

(1) For answers to our prayers for the salvation of those who are subjects of our prayers.

(2) The deepening of the spiritual life of believers, by our prayers, our preaching, the example and influence of our godly living, and through the medium of such printed matter that God may lead us to publish or distribute.

(3) Meetings for waiting on God for the Baptism with the Holy Ghost with signs following.

(4) To perpetuate as a part of our testimony, the call and commission of the church in the healing of the body through faith in the name of Jesus, the casting out of demons, and the exercise of the gifts of the Holy Ghost as the dispensational endowment of Christ our Risen Head to His Mystical Body — the Church.

(5) Faith in God for the supply of all the temporal needs of the home and the personal needs of the workers.

(6) A missionary channel — in the ministry of intercession, and such temporal gifts that we be made stewards of, for that purpose.

(7) To make the home a home of rest and quiet for God's people seeking spiritual and physical ministries.

(8) The cooperation of all the residents of the home in the life of faith, and work, and business of the home.

(9) Above all, the practice of perfect love, and the mind of Christ, in meekness of spirit, and lowliness of heart, towards all.

(10) Witness to the near coming of our Lord Jesus to reign as King over all the earth, and the necessary preparation of His waiting and watching ones to meet Him at Him coming.

Our hearts as well as the home have been open to all whom God has sent to us to receive the ministries of the home, without charge.

[See Appendix B for a sermon by Rev. Reuben A. Gibson.]

Excerpts from Sister Christine Gibson's article, *What Hath God Wrought!*, follow:

> "And I will shake all nations, and the desire of all nations shall come: and I will fill this house with glory, saith the Lord of hosts. The silver is mine, and the gold is mine, saith the Lord of hosts. The glory of this latter house shall be greater than of the former, saith the Lord of hosts: and in this place will I give peace, saith the Lord of Hosts"
> (Haggai 2:7-9).

This was the word of the Lord to us at the time we took charge of the home, and although we have not as yet seen the full glory of the home, there has been so much accomplished in two years that our hearts are filled with praise and gratitude to Him for His faithful dealings with us, and we are encouraged to trust Him for the fulfillment of all His promises to us. For His glory, and the blessing it may be to others, we mention some of His gracious dealings with us, and a few of the remarkable answers to prayer.

Just about a month after we had taken charge of the home, the interest on the mortgage became due (the home is mortgaged for $3,000). At this time we had not a penny to meet it with. We were receiving, through the freewill offerings from week to week, only enough to buy food. This was to be our first test in our work of faith, but our faithful God rose up to the occasion and met us in a very blessed way. He was testing our faith, and this only that He might develop it. Strong faith can only come through severe testings.

One day after a season of much prayer concerning the matter, an elderly lady and her niece called at the home to inquire for a Mrs. S. who had been with us but had left the week before. The aunt seemed somewhat troubled in not finding Sister S. at the home, and, in the course of conversation, we found out the cause of her trouble. She said her niece needed help, and she thought that, had she found her friend with us, Sister S. might have been able to help her. We questioned the niece and found that she was afflicted in body and mind. The Lord revealed to myself and my husband the nature of the affliction. We rose up and rebuked the oppressing spirit. The young lady was wonderfully delivered, and at the aunt's request, they remained with us in the home for a little over a week.

On the morning of their departure, the aunt placed in my hand ten dollars as a freewill offering, saying that it was all she had with her at the time. We thanked her but felt impressed to ask her to remain for the prayer service in the parlor, which she did. During that service, God worked mightily on this dear one, as we spoke of God's dealings with us in our life of faith. It moved her to make a larger offering. Her niece came to where I was kneeling and whispered in my ear that as soon as they returned home, she would send us $100.00. This was certainly "exceeding abundantly above all we had asked or thought," for the interest was only $90.00, but here was one hundred and we had already received $10.00. *Praise God!*

Not only on temporal lines has God met us and blessed us in the home, but we have also proved Him as the Faithful One on spiritual physical lines.

A very remarkable case of healing occurred during our first winter in the home. Our sister, who lives with us, and is one of the workers in the home, brought with her (having obtained our consent) a little boy about four years old which she took from the Children's Home in Rumney, New Hampshire, where she spent a few months previous to the time of our taking charge of this home.

The child was in very poor health at the time he came, and during the winter, he was stricken with a severe case of pneumonia. We did all we could for him in nursing, etc., but he kept growing worse, until it seemed as though he would surely die. Many of the saints were praying for him and the Lord very definitely led us to put our trust in Him as the only Physician for this case, and not to call an earthly doctor.

It was quite a testing time, and some of the dear ones grew very nervous over the stand we had taken, thinking that the child might die, and that we would be in trouble. But God had spoken to some of us and we felt sure that He would see us through as we obeyed Him.

One night when the child seemed to be dying, I fell on my face before the Lord and asked Him to show me definitely whether the child would live or die. The voice of the Spirit came immediately and bade me arise and take up my Bible. I did so, not knowing where I should read. I opened to John 4, and my eyes fell on these words, "Go thy way; thy son liveth" (verse 50). I felt that was God's voice to me, for, from the time he came to the home, this child called me and my husband, *Mamma and Papa*. We had looked upon him as our own child; hence, no Scripture could have been more appropriate than the one given.

I was thus freshly encouraged to believe for his healing. It was completed in two days from the time God spoke to us.

During those two days we were sorely tempted, yet that Scripture was a strong anchor to which we clung. Today the child is well and stronger than when he first came to us. He delights to tell how God healed him, quoting often the Scripture given to us: *God told Mamma "Go thy way; thy son liveth."*

This is the most severe case of sickness we have had in the home since we took charge, and we praise the Lord for helping us to be true to Him. It has strengthened our faith in trusting for other cases since then.

Among these was the case of a brother who came to us terribly oppressed in body and mind. For a day or two after he came, the demon in him raged. Some in the home were greatly scared, but God had given us His Word, *This kind goeth out by nothing but prayer and fasting.* Therefore, we knew that if we met the conditions, deliverance would come, and that there was nothing to fear since our God was stronger than the devil. Accordingly, some of us fasted, prayed with the brother, and rebuked the spirit that was tormenting him. Although the battle waged hard for some time, deliverance finally came and he returned home healed and with a sound mind. *Hallelujah!*

The interest of the mortgage was again due, and as with the others, we had no money on hand to meet it. However, because our Father had been so faithful to us in the past payments, we were not at all disturbed when it first came due. The month closed; others followed, until three months had passed with yet no sign of the money; and we grew somewhat anxious. The mortgage holder wanted his money. We prayed earnestly about it but the test continued until the fourth month. It was then that the word of the Lord came to us.

A revelation was first given to my husband. He told me about it the next day. This sent me to my knees to find out God's will for me in the matter, for I knew that God put us together in this work of faith, and I desired to work harmoniously with my companion. Husband said that God had shown him that instead of praying as we had formerly done for the interest money, we were to cooperate with Him for the removing of the mortgage from the home. He also told me that God had shown him a plan whereby it could be done.

But, of course, this plan for raising mortgage money did not seem to answer the question about the interest money which was now long overdue. I was still perplexed.

Whilst on my knees, this Scripture was given, "Faith without works is dead" (James 2:20b). While meditating on it, I was shown that the works of faith are obedience, as illustrated by Abraham and Rahab, the harlot. Abraham was justified when he offered up Isaac in obedience to God's word. Rahab was saved through obeying the words of the spies, in hanging out the scarlet line. The Spirit then reminded me of the word that was given to us when we first took charge: "Be strong...and work" (Haggai 2:4).

I was then shown that my work was to obey the word of God to me — whenever it was given, and whatever it required me to do. I got no further light that day, but I rose up with a determination to obey

God at any cost and to stand with my husband in all that God had shown him at that time.

A day or two afterwards, whilst on the train to Boston, I had a mental vision of a sister I had met a few times in Pentecostal assemblies. With the vision, these thoughts came: *That sister will help you in the present need of the home, but you will have to make it known to her, just as Elijah had to go to the widow and tell her to make him a little cake, etc.*

At first, I shrank from this, for it was so different from any of His past dealings with us in the home. We had never gone to any one about our needs. God had always sent them to us. However, I had promised obedience at any cost, so I made up my mind that I would obey just as soon as I was thoroughly convinced that this was the voice of God speaking to me.

I shared this vision with my husband and was surprised to find that this woman and her husband had been laid on his heart, too. He had met this sister's husband several times and felt that they would be interested in helping our work of faith. This strengthened my conviction, and as we waited before the Lord, my husband saw in a vision a five-dollar bill and felt impressed to pay my fare to the city where this couple lived. We placed this matter before the Lord, as a test, and two days later, we received five dollars in the mail. Although we had never visited their city, nor even knew which part of the city they lived in, I took the train that afternoon in obedience to the word of God.

I reached the city at 7:20 p.m. and found their address in a directory. I inquired about the street cars

The Exercise of Faith 99

and was told which one would take me to this lady's home. It seemed like a venturesome trip, for I didn't even know if they would be home when I got there, because they traveled a good deal. However, I felt sure that God would see the matter through if it was of Him, and I knew that I would not be disappointed.

The car stopped and the conductor told me that I had reached the avenue. I got off and was surprised to find myself in the woods. It was very dark and I knew not where to go. As I prayed, the Lord directed my steps. I was walking toward a light when I heard footsteps, and I felt that I was to stop until that person got near, and then to inquire of him. This I did.

This was truly God's leading, for the person (a gentleman) knew all about the place and the people I was looking for. He told me that I had gotten off at the wrong side of the avenue, but that he would take me to the house. We had to walk together some distance through the woods.

I reached the house, rang the doorbell and found the husband at home. His wife arrived later. I told my errand just as God had commanded me, and left the results with Him.

These dear ones treated me very kindly. I had a good night's rest, and the next morning, after having breakfast with them, I got ready to return home. The sister handed me a check for twenty-five dollars, saying that it was all she was shown to give. At the same time, the husband asked me for my husband's name, saying that he would send him a check for fifty dollars. I felt that God was going to use them to give the $90.00 for interest money, but here was only

$75.00. However, I kept on believing, for I knew that with God, nothing is impossible.

I left their home with checks for $75.00 and $5.00 towards my fare, plus a new pair of shoes, given to me by the kind brother. A day after I returned home, this same man wrote us a letter and enclosed $15.00, the balance due on the interest. So, *Hallelujah!* After much testing, my husband was at last able to meet the mortgage holder and pay him the interest money due.

Now we are believing that the Lord will help us in lifting the mortgage, thus freeing the home from this terrible load that it has carried for years.

I have endeavored to give a true report of God's faithful dealings with us since we took charge two years ago. My earnest prayer is that it may be made a blessing to those who read it.

At present, there are about eighteen of us in the home. We can say, to the glory of God, that from the time we were shown that we were to buy everything for cash, and not have any credit, we have done so. Today we do not owe a grocer's bill. Our food supplies are paid for day by day as God sends the money. What we cannot buy, we do without.

There are two bills which we have not been able to fully pay since we stopped crediting. One is a plumber's bill and the other a milk bill, but we are trusting that even before this report is sent out, we shall be able to pay those bills.

We have been enabled to paper and paint several rooms in the home; also, to put a nice stove in the kitchen, plus new floors in the hallway and kitchen. *To God be all the glory!*

We have a company of consecrated workers with us. No one receives a salary, but they trust God to supply their needs. Again and again, sacrifices have been made by the workers as they have given from the funds that the Lord has sent for their personal needs.

"Not unto us, O Lord, not unto us, but unto thy name give glory, for thy mercy, and for thy truth's sake"
(Ps. 115:1).

[See Appendix C for Faith Home Reports, 1913-1915.]

Chapter 15
Holding Fast the Confidence

> "Wherefore I also, after I heard of your faith in the Lord Jesus and love unto all the saints, cease not to give thanks for you"
>
> (Eph. 1:15,16).

The sacrifices of the many saints of God who stood with the Gibsons in the early days made the vision of Zion Bible Institute become a reality. There are many, many names, but only a few can be listed here. There are many who stand out in some of the existing early accounts, and in the memories of those to whom Sister Gibson related her experiences.

Among the many names prominent as benefactors, prayer warriors, supporters, and associates in those days, we find Mrs. George (Alice) Carpenter; Mr. and Mrs. Cushing and family; Mr. and Mrs. Trimm and family; Mr. and Mrs. Nelson from Fitchburg, Massachusetts; Rev. William Mitchell of Everett; Mr. and Mrs. H.T. Carpenter of Worcester; and Mrs. Eliza Comrie and her family. The list could go on to include hundreds more who are listed, I am sure, in God's great book of the faithful — such names never to be forgotten nor their sacrifices unrewarded.

To call attention to a few of these saints is difficult, lest we leave out so many others. However, as we mention some, they will serve as examples of faith and faithfulness, calling others to remembrance. Prominent in the story of Zion is the name of the Rev. Albert A. Augat, a long-time friend of the

Gibsons. Brother Augat pastored a church in Concord, New Hampshire, later living in Connecticut with his brother who was also a pastor. He came often to visit the Gibsons and served as guest preacher in the services. For many years he filled the pulpit for Sister Gibson while she ministered around the country. He later was elected to the board of Faith Home.

On August 1, 1929, Brother Augat founded the first Pentecostal Church of Taunton, Massachusetts, now the Taunton Assembly of God. He also was on the board of directors of Zion Bible Institute at the time of its first dated charter on April 16, 1941. His beneficence and services to the work will be remembered as long as the story of Zion is told.

About 1918, Sister Gibson established a children's home within the walls of Faith Home. Her sister, Alice, managed this ministry. In 1927 the operation of the children's home was moved nearby to 46 Leonard Avenue, where it remained in operation until 1938.

The vision for a Pentecostal training school was revealed to Sister Gibson, and the burden had long been on her heart. She longed to see a place where men and women, without natural means of support, could train for the Christian ministry. The fulfillment of this vision was to come in stages, or step by step, as she so often described the walk of faith. But, in the midst of the plans, a tragedy struck.

Brother Reuben Gibson, who was thought by all to become the leader and main teacher in the Bible school, was smitten with Bright's disease. For eighteen months he was sick, and countless prayers for his recovery were offered all over the country. However, his work on earth was done, and God took him to a Better Land.

Sister Gibson was deeply perplexed for a time in the face of such a tremendous responsibility. Uncertainty wavered her usually unshakeable faith. God used the Rev. Meyer Tan Ditter at this time, to reaffirm her vision for a Bible school. His account, written in 1924 before the school opened in the fall, and published in June, 1925, is both thrilling and prophetic:

> My heart became very sorrowful when I heard of the passing away of our dear Brother Gibson. This sorrow prompts me to write this article. I shall never forget the first time I met Brother Gibson. I was deeply impressed at the way he understood and expounded the blessed Word of God. I said to him one day (that was in 1922 while the Wellesley Campmeeting was going on), "Would it not be a blessing, should the Lord open a Bible school in the New England states?" And he answered, "It surely would." I have never forgotten those words. I felt that his heart was hungry to tell others about the blessed Word of God. For it was his greatest desire, and nothing pleased him better than to have a band of earnest seekers around him studying the Word of God.
>
> It was at that time that I also was hungering and thirsting to know more of God's Holy Word. I felt that nothing in the world would satisfy me better than to know the Bible. I also wanted others to know it, and felt that I must know it first before I could teach others. I was saved just a short time and had a little Bible training, but, oh, my heart was crying out for a deeper knowledge of His Word, and I realized, as never before, the great need in my life. I was doing — here and there — a little evangelistic work, yet my whole desire was to be able to teach God's Word. I will pass over many instances and experiences which God took me through to show me the need of a deep

knowledge of His Word and tell of my visit to East Providence.

I went to East Providence the first time to attend a convention which was being held on the Faith Home grounds, and while I was there, I saw a building being erected for future conventions, as the small chapel could not accommodate the large crowds attending the conventions. I never dreamed at that time what God was doing and how He was beginning to work.

I was not a stranger to those in charge of the meeting, as we had become acquainted through the Bible readings I had given while at Wellesley Camp. I was, therefore, asked to give some Bible teaching at this convention, which I did, and which the Lord blessed to many. Time went on, and in the meanwhile, God was working. I traveled everywhere, giving some studies on the Bible until I finally landed in Worcester, Massachusetts where God seemed to hold me, and there I accepted the pastorate of a Pentecostal assembly where I am still pastor, and will remain until the Lord opens the way for my future.

And now I will state my vision and conviction. I was riding through East Providence with an automobile party not long ago and stopped and visited the Faith Home. I went through the new building they were then getting ready for the recent convention. And as I walked through, God spoke to me in a vision. I was shown a school and several students studying. I could see young lives being prepared for the several fields in God's vineyard. Also a place where lives were being taught in the Word of God, thus equipping them for the Master's service. I kept this to myself for future development.

I came back to Worcester, and that vision so haunted me, that one night I could not sleep until I had written a letter which I typed the next morning and mailed to Sister Gibson. In due time, I received a reply which was not very satisfactory to me. I, therefore, dismissed it from my mind and went about my daily pastoral duties.

Sometime after that, I received a letter from Sister Gibson asking me to come to East Providence and help her in the convention which was about to begin. I felt led to go and made plans for it. One day whilst there, I talked with Sister Gibson regarding my vision. I did not know how she felt about it, or how she would take it, but the burden was heavy upon me and the only way to get it off was to talk it out with her and let her know how I felt, and what God showed me. I endeavored to show her that these were not my plans nor ideas, neither was it for a selfish purpose, but that God had put [them] upon me, and that I was going to be held responsible were I not true to the vision. In my simple way I showed her the great possibilities should such a school be opened.

In the midst of my conversation, the Holy Spirit came upon her mightily so that she fairly jumped out of her seat and exclaimed several times, "I feel the witness!" She then told how her dear husband felt about this school and how his greatest desire was that such a school be erected for the honor and glory of God. All that day she was under such an anointing of the Spirit, no one could deny that God was in the whole thing.

We soon got together and with the Lord as our Guide, began to make plans for the pushing forward of this school. It is possible to get a vision from God to do a certain thing and yet fail to carry it out. But my prayer is that this call from God will so grip all who read this article, that nothing will hinder the school from coming into being, a place where God will be honored and glorified. I ask all who read this to take the matter upon their heart, for God has spoken it. Shall He not do it? He has promised, and will He not bring it to pass? We will need your cooperation by prayer and by giving. We therefore plead with all the dear ones to unite with us in praying this thing, for Jesus sake.

God used this confirming vision as encouragement to Sister Gibson, and He also spoke directly to her in personal dealings.

In 1924, a consecrated Christian artist, Mr. Nordlen of Windsor, Vermont, was commissioned to paint the mural on the front wall of the new church. On the first panel, he was inspired to paint the open Bible with the following quotations:

"He sent His Word, and healed them, and delivered them from their destructions"
(Ps. 107:20).

"Oh, that men would praise the Lord for His goodness, and for His wonderful works to the children of men"
(Ps. 107:21).

Crowning the Book of books were these words, "Search the Scriptures." Through the years, the Holy Bible would be revered, honored, preached, and studied at Zion. Over and over again, the Scriptures would be searched, and in so doing, light would come in place of darkness; faith, in place of fear; love, in place of hate; and the peace that passeth all understanding would rest upon His people.

The artist reserved the middle panel for the cross, with a crown of jagged thorns. The words, "It is finished," were painted above it. The immortal utterance of our Redeemer, together with the cross, constantly reminded all who saw it, of the price paid for the redemption of mankind.

The time was at hand for the painting of the third panel, and no particular inspiration came to the artist. He called for Rev. Christine A. Gibson who was still co-pastor of the church with her husband. She hastened from the room of her critically ill companion, Rev. Reuben A. Gibson, and came to the tabernacle.

Together, Christine and Reuben had announced the opening of the Bible school that coming fall. It was a severe blow to have Brother Gibson so ill, for he was the one upon whom Sister Gibson depended so heavily, since he was a brilliant Bible scholar and an able administrator. With these thoughts revolving in her mind, Sister Gibson stood at the back of the church as she gazed down at the third panel.

As she looked, God gave her a vision of a casket at the front of the church, and she was made to understand that her beloved husband would not get well, but would soon be called to his eternal home. Continuing to look, she heard the blessed Holy Spirit whispering within, *"Are you willing to drink the cup?"*

Christine bowed her heart in submission and replied, "Not my will, but Thine be done." To ever remind her of this consecration, and to stimulate faith in others, she asked the artist to paint "the cup" and to place the words over it that the Master had uttered in the deepest agony of His soul while in the Garden of Gethsemane, "Thy will be done."

The beautiful mural was completed in May of 1924 and the first service held in the new church was the funeral of Rev. Reuben A. Gibson. However, the golden cup and the divine words above gave comfort and encouraged Sister Gibson as she looked upon the third panel. Not only was solace given to her, but through the years, help and sustenance have come to those who have looked at the cup and repeated the words above it.

Years later when the tabernacle became too small and the new temple was built at Zion, many changes were made, but one thing remained the same — the front mural. Brother Nordlen had passed on, but Rev. Walter Crawford, a gifted artist and minister of the Gospel, painted exactly the same words and the same mural. Thus, in every service the congregation can see the open Bible, the thorn-crowned cross, and the glistening cup, each with its own wealth of meaning — not only to Zionians, but to thousands who pass through the temple doors from year to year.

The loss of Brother Gibson was a crushing experience to Sister Gibson, but she stated, "We will ever remember Calvary, for out of a death, Zion Bible Institute was born."

As scheduled, in the fall of 1924, Zion Bible Institute opened its doors for training to help fulfill the prophecy that Zion shall be the joy of the whole earth. God sent help by bringing Miss Alice Chase back from Kentucky to stay at Zion permanently. She was faithful to Sister Gibson until the time God took Zion's founder Home to her eternal reward. Sister Chase was her personal secretary, confidante, and companion for many years. Her God-given musical talent was long a blessing as she beautifully played the piano and organ at Zion through the years.

God also sent Rev. and Mrs. Tan Ditter to help, with Brother Tan Ditter being one of the three teachers the first year that Zion opened. Along with Brother Tan Ditter and Sister Gibson, a kindly brother from Cambridge, Massachusetts, Elder George Phillips, came in weekly to teach. A long-time friend and co-worker, Rev. Kathleen (Fischer) Goodwin, was a valuable assistant and a close companion during those first years. God continued to raise up workers whom He sent to meet needs at Zion in His appointed time.

Sister Gibson did not fully realize the great plan with which God had entrusted her when she opened what was unofficially called "Mount Zion Bible School" during that first year. The first few years were difficult and at times, Sister Gibson wondered if she should go on in the face of the opposition that cried loud and long many times. With her courage, determination, and faith in God, she continued.

The second year the school was officially named "The School of the Prophets," referring to the many sons of the prophets who are mentioned in the account of Elijah and Elisha. This name remained until 1936 when it was renamed Zion Bible Institute, in accordance with the divine instruction and prophecy that the name Zion be as a covering over every building and that Zion shall be the joy of the whole earth.

Although many trials and hardships crossed her pathway and daunted her faith, Sister Gibson overcame, leaning on the strength of her Savior. Year after year, the doors were flung open, without discrimination, without limitation. No charges of any kind were placed upon the students. They came, and everyone trusted God to supply the needs of Zion. Were it not for the stand that she took, many would have been denied the privilege of Bible school training. Sister Gibson championed the rights of the poor, and the rights of all men to study the Word of God.

The doors remain open today, and from the first three students of that first year, Zion grew until presently several hundred graduates have completed their three-year course and may be found the world over, serving as pastors, missionaries, teachers, and youth workers. Each one has come under the same policy that was introduced to the first three students — faith in a living God and His immutable Word.

Chapter 16
Great Is Thy Faithfulness

"Remembering without ceasing your work of faith, and labor of love, and patience of hope in our Lord Jesus Christ, in the sight of God and our Father"
(1 Thess. 1:3).

In reviewing the very early days of Zion Bible Institute, one might well ask, "For who hath despised the day of small things?" (Zech. 4:10). One might answer, "Where there is no vision, the people perish" (Prov. 29:18). Zion Bible Institute is the result of vision.

Some years before the vision came to pass, God revealed His will concerning Faith Home and the work connected with it. This included a school of faith where consecrated young people would come to study the Word of God, and while doing so, they would get a deeper knowledge of God and learn a walk of faith.

The first vision was given to Rev. Alpheus Cleveland for a Faith Home. Later, when Rev. and Mrs. Reuben A. Gibson became managers of the home, a further revelation was given to them in regard to a school. At that time it seemed impossible to have a school — perhaps it was not God's time, for every vision is for an appointed time, they knew.

The weeks sped along into years, during which time, starting from one building known as Faith Home, the establishment grew to four buildings by 1932. A chapel was built on the grounds and then later a tabernacle was started, remaining unfinished for a time. There were no funds, and just a few workers, but the vision of a Bible school remained.

In 1923, the Lord began to work in a most unusual way. In the latter part of that year, and in the early months of 1924, it was evident that He had risen up to fulfill His word, and that the vision would speak. God heard prayer, needed funds and workers came, and the auditorium, halls and work on the lower part of the building were finished and ready for revival services on May 1, 1924.

As previously stated, a dark hour followed immediately when the Lord took Brother Gibson Home on May 5, 1924, leaving Sister Gibson to carry on alone. This nearly overwhelmed her. But as God spoke peace to her perplexed heart and instructed her to go on with His work, she obeyed.

God ministered to her in a very special way on one occasion when she was alone in her apartment, shortly after her husband's homegoing. She was missing him, feeling sad, and wondering how she could go on. All of a sudden, she felt pressure, almost like that of a person pressing up very, very close to her. Then the words, "Thy Maker is thine husband," from the 54th chapter of Isaiah, were given to her by the precious Holy Spirit. She knew that the pressure was indicative of the nearness of God himself, and after that time, this portion of Scripture was very dear to her. She took each day by faith, leaning on the Lord.

It wasn't only the words, "Thy Maker is thine husband," that meant so much to her, but also many other beautiful promises contained in this chapter. In the years that followed, she overcame great opposition and many difficulties as she led her people in the way of faith. Her Maker was, indeed, "the band around her dwelling place," and together, Christine and her closest Companion led Zion on to deeper depths and higher heights, developing a Zion family that truly cannot be numbered.

In the fall of 1924 the Bible school opened. There were a few from "outside," and along with them, most of the workers on the grounds joined in the study of the Word of God. Mrs. Lillian Wightman, secretary of the church and long-time friend of the work, came to serve as matron. God sent Rev. Meyer Tan Ditter to teach, and he and his wife lived in two rooms that were furnished in the tabernacle building. Elder George Phillips came from Massachusetts weekly to teach a class in Typology. Sister Gibson taught classes on several subjects. God worked supernaturally that first year and classes often turned into mighty demonstrations of God's power and revelation. It seems as though the group had entered a prophets' school, indeed.

School opened the second year more officially and with a larger enrollment. Marion L. Hodgeman, an English teacher, joined the faculty to teach several subjects. The curriculum became more extensive and outside ministries were begun. In those days, morning prayers were held in the reception hall of the tabernacle, and how the power of God did fall! Many times God revealed His plan in definite matters pertaining to the work, as well as answering prayers for great needs. Sister Gibson gave choice exhortations which were of deep spiritual benefit. Many problems and many testings came as the enemy tried to thwart God's plans, but God took Zion through victoriously.

In 1927, the children's home ministry expanded by enlarging the chapel to care for children of sincere Christian workers. One of the workers who had children in the home was Kathleen Fischer who desired an opportunity to study the Word of God. The children's home was in charge of Mrs. Wilbert Rich, mentioned elsewhere in this book as Alice, Sister Gibson's sister. This department was also a part of the vision from God.

A third floor was eventually added to Faith Home to accommodate young women. God provided for these enlargements as the people trusted Him. Stewards were raised up. Because it was a faith school, no sum was charged to any student. Many students had to learn to trust God for individual needs as they had no one else to look to for personal support. Also, they saw opportunities to share with others who were in need. Even the ordinary work was shared by all, and students were trained to be practical Christian workers. In a variety of ways, the Lord supplied food for all three departments of the work at Zion, but especially noted here is the provision for the school.

In 1927, Sister Gibson and a party of workers were invited to attend a convention at the Mars Hill Full Gospel Assembly in Mars Hill, Maine. Sister Gibson was asked to be the Bible teacher during the convention. She had met the pastor, Rev. Harold Bickford, at the Wellesley Park gathering, and he had invited her to Mars Hill. Sister Gibson and her friends spread a map out on the living room floor at Faith Home and looked and looked, followed and followed, until they finally found the little town of Mars Hill, Maine, on the map. It was just a small spot in the center of Aroostook County, Maine.

It seemed very far away, and at that time, it was. There were no lovely turnpikes or special highways, and it took quite some time to get there. However, Sister Gibson felt very strongly that she should accept this invitation. They arrived and God blessed the services. They made many new friends and led people to the Lord, helping bring them into the wonderful baptism of the Holy Spirit. All too quickly it was time for the meetings to close.

Brother Bickford felt sad because the economy was not good and a great depression was about to fall upon the country.

He didn't know just where he was going to get an honorarium of worthy proportions to give to this Gospel party. However, Mrs. Bickford rose, went to the platform, and said, "We don't have money, but we do have a very special product here. This is Aroostook County and our main crop is potatoes. I feel that we should give the school, of which Sister Gibson is the leader, a freight carload of potatoes." This suggestion was unanimously received by the people and potato houses became a flurry of activity.

After Sister Gibson had been home awhile, she received word from the railroad station that a carload of potatoes had arrived. She sent young men to the station with burlap bags and baskets. They unloaded the potatoes and brought them back to the cellar which had been specially prepared to keep them as they ought to be kept.

Now, in 1992, as this little resume of Sister Gibson's life is being recorded, I can say that every year since then, the dear saints of Aroostook County, Maine, have sent potatoes to Zion. These Maine potatoes have been received with gratitude, and what a help they have been in preparing meals for all who live at Zion. Of course, they don't arrive in freight cars now — they come in beautiful, sleek, silver trucks which glide into the school parking lot very easily.

The potatoes arrive in bags, and, as always, a group of young male students unload and store them.

We acknowledge with gratefulness the faithful generosity of Mr. Gary Bell, a well-known potato farmer in Mars Hill, Maine. He continues to supply the bulk of the potatoes to the school, along with portions from other farmers. The Lord is the only One who has a list of all the contributing farmers, and we wish that we had a copy of it here, so that we could list them all. However, those who have given in secret shall receive their rewards openly. This, God has promised!

At times it was a day at a time, trusting, trusting. One day a barrel of sugar came from a friend in Hartford, Connecticut; fresh vegetables came form the gardens of various friends; and God raised up Lyman G. Hoxie of Raynham, Massachusetts, who owned a fruit orchard, to be one of God's stewards in the early days of Zion.

At a time of great need, a whole truckload of canned goods and vegetables came from western New York State. This was quite an experience. We had gone down into the dining room for our evening meal, and actually there wasn't that much to eat. Sister Gibson rose and said, "Let us sing the Doxology."

The group rose and sang, "Praise God from Whom all blessings flow," and then there was a sound of clattering on the stairs. One of the older saints came down, burst into the room, and exclaimed, "Come! Come!" A young man followed her down and announced that they were from western New York State and that he had a truckload of canned goods, staples, groceries, fruits, and much more. Supper had come — God's blessings were flowing! The group waited a little while and a delicious meal was served. Beyond that, that young man presented Sister Gibson with money in an envelope. This is just one example of the many ways in which the Lord wonderfully met the needs of Zion time and time again.

Rev. D. Paul Longstreth, missionary to Africa, visited Faith Home and the school around the end of 1928. His impression of this work follows:

> Since coming to Faith Home, I have come in contact with some real saints of God. My stay here has certainly been a great blessing to me, both

spiritually and temporally. I must say, for the glory of God, this is the most spiritual place I have been in, for sometime.

On Sunday morning, the word of the Lord came forth through messages of tongues and interpretation, and was a great encouragement to me. I truly praise the Lord, because there are the few here and there who are paying the price, and are going through with God.

I certainly like the method which Sister Gibson and the teachers have adopted in teaching the students. The Lord bless them for their efforts. They have a fine body of students who are on fire for God, and want God's best, whatever it might be.

The work in general, which is being carried on entirely by faith, is a grand memorial to the Lord.

The visit and spiritual blessing which I received here, will always remain in my mind. May the Lord richly bless dear Sister Gibson and all the others for their kindness to me, is the prayer of my heart.

A newspaper article records a revival at Zion Tabernacle:

Since the start of the 1929-30 term of the School of the Prophets on November 4, a revival spirit has fallen upon Zion Tabernacle at 846 Broadway.

There are 21 students enrolled in the Bible school. A number of them have started an orchestra to furnish music for the services in Zion Tabernacle.

Mrs. C.A. Gibson is the pastor of the Tabernacle and also the principal of the Bible School.

The meetings are as follows: Sunday school at 9:45 a.m.; morning worship at 10:45 a.m.; and evangelistic at 7 p.m. On Tuesday evening at 7:30, a tarrying service is held for those desiring the Baptism of the Holy Spirit. On Friday evenings at 7:30, a praise and prayer service is held. The public is invited to attend the services.

The students enrolled are Luella Belmont, Rochester, N.Y.; Florence Craig, Mars Hill, Me.; Laura Crookshanks, Newark, Del.; Marie E. Dyer, Rockport, Me.; Lily Ericson, Hartford, Conn.; Mary Fifer, Boston, Mass.; Muriel Grant, New York City; Dorothy Marshall, Portland, Me.; Henrietta May, Moffatt, Ont., Canada; Pearl McDermott, Tilley, N.B., Canada; Helen J. Pierce, Westfield, Me.; Sidney Reed, Bethel, Conn.; Phyllis Tuttle, Biddeford, Me.; Gladys S. Wall, Hartford, Conn.; Irving Cole, Ashland, Me.; William J. Hollyer, Worcester, Mass.; Raymond Miller, Mendon, Mass.; Henry Nicoliason, Tottenville, N.Y.; Henry Sinclair, New Haven, Conn.; Samuel Thompson, Camden, N.J.; and William K. Wilson, Mars Hill, Me.

The musicians in the orchestra are Irvin Cole, cornetist; Sidney Reed, cornetist; William G. Hollyer, piccolo; Mary Fifer, violinist; Lily Ericson, violinist; Gladys S. Wall, saxaphonist; William K. Wilson, trombonist; and Miss Alice Chase, pianist.

In 1930, the enrollment numbered forty-four students. They came from many states. The morning chapel hours were times of great refreshing from the Lord. There was evidence of a real revival. Sacrifices were made and God moved upon many to meet the financial needs of the work.

Aaron Kelly from Caribou, Maine, was a first year student in the fall of 1930. He recorded his impressions:

We shall always remember the spiritual influence that our Spirit-filled teachers exerted upon our lives. At the pinnacle of our regard, stands Sister Christine Gibson, our principal, teacher, and friend. I speak for our class: We have found her a woman of God with the love and compassion of Christ flooding her heart and soul. She has been impartial in her relationships with each of us, lending a helping hand to the weak, and standing in prayer with the discouraged ones who might otherwise have fallen. She felt with us, and worked with us, with one aim — to please her God, and to fulfill her mission as co-worker with Him. We also cannot forget Sister Eleanor Berchtold and Brother Russell Goodwin. Personal contact with these teachers added much to the spirituality and inspiration of our freshman year.

The children's home was completed in 1927, and in 1931 God met Zion with another challenge. More accommodations were needed for the increasing number of students. Rose Corey (later Rose Rojas) came to Zion and told how the Lord had laid it upon her heart to make a gift of $1,000.00 to erect a utility building. This building was to consist of garages below and rooms for sleeping quarters above, plus one classroom. (In later years the garages were removed and a large classroom replaced them.) The Lord indicated through a manifestation of the Spirit that it should be built at once. This called for a greater exercise of faith and more prayer. Nonetheless, Sister Gibson, truly a woman of vision and sacrifice, was equal to it. As her faithful workers held together with her, God did not fail. The building was soon finished and school opened with fifty-three students. Rose Corey enrolled and God saw her through, even to the mission field in Colombia, South America, where she met her husband. She was well repaid in many ways for her sacrifice.

The year 1930 was the first "real" graduation ceremony that Zion held. Earlier students were merely given diplomas.

The increase in students necessitated enlarging and repainting the dining room. God provided the funds for this. Faithful workers gave their services in the culinary department. Many of these folks have gone on to their heavenly reward, but we thank God for every one of them. We name a few here: Sister Hope Stocker, Sister Ruth Simpson-Gowell, Sister Louise Lamb, Rev. Walter Bouchard, Sister Doris Snyder, and on and on we could go. Brother Bouchard received a good training in faith and it helped him when he established his own work among the French-speaking people in Montreal, Quebec, Canada. Every worker, in turn, has contributed his individual talents to the service of the Lord with no apparent thought of reward.

Those were wonderful days — days when the treasury was often empty and 100 people on the ground who had to be fed — but they were days when God performed miracles right before our eyes. Often the Zion family would gather in the dining hall to pray, each one looking to the Lord, for we all were totally dependent upon Him for our supplies. Sometimes the answer came in the mail, other times through a friend, and sometimes a stranger would visit, and seeing the need, would meet it himself. Or, the phone would ring with a message, "I have an offering and the Lord has shown me that you have a special need."

It comes to mind, as I'm thinking of the mail, that there was a day in the history of Zion when the Providence Gas Company sent one of its workers to turn off the gas at Zion. The bill was very large at that time, and Sister Gibson asked him if he would mind waiting a few hours. She did this, knowing in her heart that money might come in the mail. The man said that he would be back. In the meantime, the mail came and as

Sister Gibson looked through her letters, she exclaimed, "Oh, dear, here is a letter from Richard (Dick) Yonkers, a missionary, way over in India." (He had been a student prior to his going to India and she hardly expected an offering from this missionary.) But, nevertheless, she opened the envelope and what do you suppose fell out? It was a money order in the exact amount necessary to pay the gas bill. The matter was taken care of and the gas was not turned off. Since then, utilities have not been discontinued at Zion, even to this present day.

The Lord showed how He could supply Zion's needs in various ways through the years. He taught us that we cannot get our eyes on one particular person, or on one outstanding organization. We are to look to Him. In many ways, our manner of doing business has had to change because of the times in which we live, but God has never changed. The work at Zion has grown and grown and God is still taking care of it in some of these unusual ways.

He often gave us the desires of our hearts. Every holiday we had special dinners — like turkey and all the fixings — and He has never failed the Zion family once. It has been a step-by-step walk in faith. We are confident that the God who began the work is sufficiently able to perform that which He has set His hand to do.

In 1932, sixty-three students were enrolled. As the years passed, many young people, men, and women were trained. Many talented and consecrated workers have been sent forth into the vineyard of our Master, both here and abroad. The missionary department of Zion alone brought forth many tireless laborers, such as Bill and Mary (Fifer) Wilson, Willard and Florence Wilson, Leon and Almeida Elliot, Marguerite Watson, Celia Piper, Leslie and Mildred Bedell, and countless others. Some did not remain long on the field because of ill health.

Gertrude Bailey went happily to South America, but illness came upon her and she had to be brought home. Louise Lamb, who cooked so long in Zion's kitchen, making good cakes, pies, cookies, and more, went down into the Kentucky mountains and labored there for some time. Mary Carle went to Egypt and was plagued by illness, so she had to return after a few years. Some of these people have gone on to be with the Lord, and I feel that their reward will be beautiful. Since these early years, younger missionaries have gone to lands afar, helping to make Zion "the joy of the whole earth."

In the fall of 1933, Mrs. Lillian Wightman was unable to continue her duties as matron, having to go home to take care of her aged father. Mrs. Luna Blanchard and Mrs. Margaret Anna Thompson took over her duties. Mrs. Thompson became the matron and she was devoted to seeing that Zion was kept clean from the cellar to the attic. Every spring, whitewash buckets appeared and the cellar was swept and whitewashed. Lace curtains came down. She had some kind of a curtain gadget that stretched lace curtains and many of the girls went around with bleeding hands, having stuck their fingers on the sharp little nails of the curtain stretchers. The place was always lovely and clean.

Mrs. Blanchard, who has been mentioned previously, was an excellent teacher, especially of the Old Testament.

Mrs. Marie King came from Washington, D.C. and was appointed dean of girls. Everyone loved and respected Sister King, and she, in turn, loved Zion and the people in it. Many who read this will recall her classes in Personal Work and Typology. She not only taught personal work, but she also lived an exemplary life of a soul winner. Sister King died at 101 years of age in February of 1991. She was lovingly cared for at Zion until she passed away. She had met Sister Gibson at a Potomac

Campmeeting in Virginia where Sister Gibson was a Bible teacher.

When Sister Gibson arrived at this camp, she thought that she had her teaching notes and other special words from the Lord with her in the car. Traveling with Sister Gibson was Sylvia Gibbs (now Sylvia Hill), her grand-niece. She turned to Sylvia and said, "Bring in that little case with my notes." However, it was then discovered that they had been left at Zion. Sister Gibson became very upset and was quite frustrated for a while, but she looked to the Lord and He gave her beautiful lessons to deliver each day. She had marvelous gifts of the Spirit, and the Lord used her in that manner, also.

It was at this camp that Sister Gibson met a beautiful woman who had a lot of dark hair, beautiful eyes, and was quite aristocratic-looking. Her name was Charlotte Marie King. She was enthralled with the messages and with the ministries. She and her family took Sister Gibson out for lunch and later on, Sister King came to Rhode Island for a convention. While in Rhode Island, Marie felt a strong tug in her heart to cast her lot with the people of Zion. She mentioned this to Sister Gibson, who, in turn, said, "No, dearie, this isn't for you. I cannot offer you a salary."

Sister King had been working at a large church in Washington, D.C., and was engaged in other things there as well. Her daughter lived in that city, also. Sister Gibson brought out these facts and tried her best to discourage Marie from joining them at Zion. However, Sister King finally convinced Sister Gibson that she knew it was the will of God. Hence, Sister Gibson invited her and she joined the Zion family in 1933. What a blessing she was to countless numbers of young people who passed through the portals of Zion Bible Institute!

In 1934 Sister Eleanor Bertchold, by now a missionary to South America, penned a tribute to Sister Gibson:

God's grace thru a broken vessel,
To us has been revealed:
In her, our precious sister,
Christ-chosen, Spirit-sealed.
Sweet fragrance of heavenly glory
Can only thus be shed
By vessels, broken and emptied of self,
And filled with the Christ, instead.
Controlled by a passionate passion for Christ,
To Him, she has ever been true;
He is her Lord, her Master, her King;
His will, she loves to do.
Like Deborah of old, she encouraged our faith
In our God, and to battle, led us on,
Never faltering, tho' the enemy pressed,
Until the victory was won.
We will follow her example,
And her faith, we'll emulate;
Then, when battles here are over,
Triumphant, sweep thru' heaven's gates.

Chapter 17
The Bugle Call Is Given

"Watch ye, stand fast in the faith, quit you like men, be strong"
(1 Cor. 16:13).

The next year brought added responsibility as ninety students were enrolled in the fall of 1934. Great sacrifices were made on the part of the students, helping to meet the needs at Zion. The children's home, with most of the children having grown older, began to be used for a ladies' dormitory.

Doris Melissa Blanchard showed her appreciation of Sister Gibson in 1934 when she wrote of her years at Zion:

> It is a pleasure to turn to Sister Gibson at this time with words of appreciation, for we know that it is because of her faith in God, and her sacrifices, that we have been enabled to receive training here.
>
> On our arrival at school, the first thing to meet our eyes, was the inscription over the doorway, *FAITH HOME*. Blind indeed is he who has not found an atmosphere of both faith and home here. How often we have heard visitors, including students from other schools, comment upon the home-like atmosphere. This is all due to the motherly attitude which Sister Gibson has taken, toward her big family, for such we have become.

How often we've had to take the humble path and say "forgive me" to each other, for a misdemeanor, or an ill-spoken word. Will we ever forget our fellowship together? We've been through hard places, and surmounted obstacles, which then seemed so hard and trying, but we've gone through them together.

It is Sister Gibson who has kept a watchful eye over us, with the help of the Lord, guiding us over treacherous, foreboding places.

No matter how far the path of life leads us from Faith Home, we shall never forget our days in the School of the Prophets. Remembering our days here will bring to mind the one who has held the fort so long and so faithfully — Sister Gibson.

It was true, Sister Gibson loved the students with the heart of a mother. Having her students graduate and leave must have been a bittersweet experience. However, she sent them out into the harvest field with her blessings:

Beloved class of 1934:

As I started to write my farewell message for your class paper, I was led to the passage of Scripture in Psalm 104:26, "There go the ships." Believing it to be God's thought for my message, I now proceed.

In fancy I picture you as a fleet of ships going forth from the dock (School of the Prophets), on God's sea of life. I seem to see the Bible school as a great shipyard where myself and the rest of the faculty have been busily engaged during the past months in the work of ship building — assisting the great Master Builder, in putting together material for forming character, and equipping you for your future ministry.

At last the hour has come, to bid you farewell and Godspeed. In vision, I am standing on the pier with the rest of the faculty, watching you as you are about to cut the shore lines and launch out into the deep. As I watch with deep interest and grave concern, serious thoughts flit through my mind: "What will become of them? Have they been firmly built, to withstand the storms and tempests which will undoubtedly meet them as they sail? Will they safely arrive some happy morning in their desired haven, or will they be shipwrecked?" Everything depends upon how the ships go.

"There go the ships!" Every ship has a captain. They cannot go of their own accord. Someone must manage the helm, regulate the sails, control the engine. All hands must be obedient to the captain's orders. What about your captain? Is Jesus on board your ship? Is He in full control? Are you ready to have Him rule all your faculties and direct your course? If so, each ship will sail prosperously, and arrive safely. It may meet with storms, but it is sure of reaching the harbor. If Christ is given His rightful place in your lives, you will consult Him in all your plans. You will consider whether your words will please Him before you speak; whether your deeds will honor Him before you act. If you do this, then He is, indeed, Captain of your ship. "There go the ships!" Every ship has a chart. The captain consults his chart and directs his course, accordingly. God's Word is your Chart, and each one of you should understand enough of it to sail rightly. When you are in doubt as to the Captain's orders, or of the perils of the sea, consult your Chart. The Bible has instructions for guidance during your entire journey. Keep your Chart, the Word of God, ever before you. Let the Bible travel with you as your loving companion. It assures you safe arrival at the other side.

"There go the ships!" What do they carry? They are surely not empty or setting idle. A few of them may be pleasure yachts. Some may be laden mostly with ballast, but, as a rule, ships on the sea carry cargo of value. What kind of cargo are you carrying? Is it poor or valuable? In other words, what is your character? The ship is built for the benefit of what it is to transmit. Life is to be lived for the sake of what it is, and what it does for others. What has the Bible school training done for you in the way of character-building? What has it done for you in the way of equipment? What have you on board to transmit to others? Have you stored up the Word of God richly in your hearts? Are you endued with power from on High, so that you can effectually give as cargo, the full Gospel to others?

Ships also carry passengers. Are you equipped to take passengers on board? It would be a pity, if, after these years of training in Bible school, you should enter into harbor with cargo of no value, and with no passengers on board. On the other hand, what a glad time it would be, if, after sailing through deep and stormy seas, meeting with tempetuous winds, you arrive safely on the other side with your cargo preserved, and with passengers on board, ready to be presented as trophies to the great Owner of all ships, and to hear His *Well done, good and faithful servants; enter into the joy of your Lord.*

"There go the ships!" God prosper them one and all. Yes, in closing, I say, *God prosper you, one and all, precious young men and women, class of 1934.* You have but one voyage to make, only one life to live — be your very best for God, and see that you do not become shipwrecked. Go forth on your voyage, with Jesus as your Captain, the Bible as your Chart, and a godly character — the result of a Spirit-filled life — as your cargo.

I wish you all a safe voyage and a happy arrival some glad morning in the beautiful haven of rest. I trust that, when you finally enter the harbor, I shall be among the number of loved ones to greet you, and to bid you "welcome home," and that together, we shall share the reward of faithful service. Go forth to the call of the hour; go "rescue the perishing and care for the dying." God bless you all. Sail on!

The following year, the roof on the dormitory was raised to provide more rooms for teachers and students, as enrollment reached 112 students.

Each student was now charged the small sum of ten dollars as an entrance fee. However, the school continued wholly on a faith basis. As Sister Gibson meditated about opening the school, year after year, and not asking for any definite sum for tuition, she felt in her spirit that she must put more responsibility upon the students who came. For that reason, she asked for a ten-dollar entrance fee.

As the work has progressed and grown, and as the economy has changed, a fee has been charged to help bear the expense of operating. However, no one has been turned away due to lack of funds who was considered eligible and had potential in the ministry.

From time to time, and from year to year, improvements were made to the buildings. Many times a former graduate of the school has supplied the money needed for improvements.

The class of 1935 was facing graduation, and its beloved leader sat again at her desk and sent them forth with endearing words:

> Dear to this heart of mine,
>
> The hour is fast approaching when we must say *Farewell.* In fancy, I see you as a company of soldiers, ready to enter the battlefield. Before the Throne, I pray that you may be ready for any call, along any road, and for any service.
>
> How well I recall your entrance into the "School of the Prophets!" You came as volunteers who had heard and answered the call to the service of your King. You came with high hopes and large expectations. In your souls burned a lofty purpose to make your lives count for God. From many paths and environments of life, you came, and your dispositions and characteristics were equally varied. Some of you seemed strong and courageous when you first entered; you were ready for anything. Confidence in your own selves was likened to that of Peter in his beginnings. Others came with unbroken spirits and wills. Some of you suffered keenly from timidity and sensitiveness. Nevertheless, all of you came, willing to be merged into one big training camp, under the "Commander-in-Chief." I have considered it a privilege, through His appointment, to have a part in your training.

Yes, joy is in my soul as I think of the time when I answered God's call to open this training camp — the Bible school. I praise Him for the many young lives that have, since that time, also responded to the call, yielded to the training, and are now out in active service for the Lord. Many of them are bringing honor to His name, and are a credit to the School.

Upon entering the camp, many of you had a rather perverted conception of what such training involved. You soon discovered that the students that were gathered here for training, were not of angelic order. They were just ordinary human beings, "subject to like passions" as yourselves. The mingling in close quarters, with a variety of dispositions and character, has been a tremendous asset in your training, for you have learned to know yourselves, and your own limitations, as never before. Such association has brought to light many things of which you were ignorant.

That which you considered strong and reliable in yourselves, seemed to wilt and fade away. The consciousness of your own nothingness was painful to endure, but it led you to cast yourselves on the all-sufficient grace of Christ. This is where you learned the fundamental lesson that is absolutely essential to the success of a Christian warrior; namely, that it is "Not by might, nor by power, but by my Spirit, saith the Lord."

The tests along physical, mental, financial, and spiritual lines have been part of your training, teaching you that, only as you conquer in today's tests, will you be ready for the greater test tomorrow. Only as you have overcome the "lion and the bear" in your private life are you equipped to go forth and slay mighty Goliaths on the battlefield.

Now, on the eve of your departure, I see myself standing beside you, ready to wave you off to the battlefield. The bugle call is given. It calls you to action. What is the message of the bugle? Listen! *Watch ye, stand fast in the faith, quit you like men, be strong!* (See 1 Cor. 16:13.) Of whom does this bugle call remind us? None other than the brave, weather-beaten Paul, the Apostle, who sounded it many years ago, to the soldiers of the early church. Paul was well-fitted to sound such a call, for had he not fought and conquered in many a battle, and did he not know perfectly the requirements of warfare?

Today the bugle call comes to you, young soldiers of the cross. It bids you, *"Keep awake!"* Every sensibility must be fully alert; every nerve, keen for battle. Only as you are fully awake, will you be sensitive to the enemy's tactics and be able to see and interpret the movements of your Commander. Tragic is the fact that men, who, at one time, fought noble battles, have accepted opiates and are now asleep. Dear students, be warned by the failures of others! Remember, the disciples miserably failed Christ when He needed them the most. Why? Because they failed to keep awake and pray during His agony in the Garden. You are going forth with a last-hour message. The clouds of sin hang heavily over the world. Let your message of light help disperse the gloom. *"Ho, watchman, what of the night?"*

The next blast from the bugle sounds forth, *"Stand fast in the faith!"* — that glorious faith "once for all, delivered to the saints." This is the faith for which early martyrs laid down their lives. Stand fast in the faith, that Jesus is "the same yesterday, today, and forever." When every circumstance and feeling would contradict faith, still "stand fast." Press the Sacred Book, with its divine promises, to your heart, and "stand fast." When other comrades compromise the truth for personal benefit, and let down the standards of our glorious Pentecostal faith, desiring popularity with the crowd, God help you to "stand fast in the faith." This faith will place all heaven's resources at your disposal.

Oh, warriors, hold high the shield of faith, as you go forth to battle! Never place it in the sheath of unbelief. Keep it ever ready for action. With it, you shall quench all the fiery darts of the enemy. With it, you shall do mighty exploits, pulling down Satan's strongholds. Through its power, you shall fight to the end, and remain victorious on the field.

Another strain from the bugle is, *Quit you like men!* The call is for men, not children. Away with childish things! Remember, you have been trained for battle. Men of sterling character and bravery are wanted. Counterfeit soldiers are exempted. Only those can be accepted who are ready to endure unto death — those who will stand in the face of disaster and bloodshed. It is an insult to our Commander to offer Him anything less than full consecration.

The last strain from the bugle is, *Be strong!* Be strong! In your prayer life, "be strong!" In your sacrifice, "be strong!" In your visions, "be strong!" In your standards, "be strong!" *Be strong!* "Be strong" in your warfare! "Be strong in the Lord and in the power of His might!"

"Where were you wounded?" asked the surgeon of a soldier at Lookout Mountain. "Almost at the top," he answered. He forgot his gaping wound; he remembered that he had won the heights. O, soldiers of Jesus Christ, let us press on. Never be satisfied until, from the very top, you can exclaim with joy, "I have fought a good fight, I have finished my course, I have kept the faith." *God bless you and keep you true to the end.*

> O, may His counsels guide, uphold you,
> 'Neath His wings protecting, hide you,
> When life's perils thick, confound you,
> Keep love's banner floating o'er you;
> God be with you till we meet again.
> (Selected)

Your loving principal and friend,
Christine A. Gibson

In 1936, the name of the school was changed from "School of the Prophets" to "Zion Bible Institute." Years before, God had called the place *Zion,* and had given many precious promises by His Spirit in connection with this name. In this same year, diplomas were awarded at graduation time in the name of Zion Bible Institute, instead of the School of the Prophets.

School records show that the year of 1939 began with an outpouring of the Spirit. Twelve students received the baptism of the Holy Spirit and at the close of the year, thirty-nine students received diplomas and went out into the harvest field to work for the Lord.

Chapter 18
Enlarge the Place of Thy Tent

> "So they strengthened their hands for this good work...for the people had a mind to work"
> (Neh. 2:18d and 4:6c).

Through the years, God has enriched Zion Bible Institute through the high caliber of the faculty as her own graduates answered the call to teach in the school, and as other qualified teachers joined the staff.

Rev. Henry Sinclair began a devoted work among the students. He was a marvelous teacher, opening up the Word of the Lord in the classroom and making it very real as his thoughts were anointed by the Holy Spirit. A great sadness came upon Zion when he was stricken with cancer. It was a fast-moving type of disease. We prayed much, but the doctor's prognosis was not good. It seemed in the planning and purpose of God that it was his time to leave us, and one day he slipped away to be with the Lord.

Rev. Albert Spaeder returned to teach and to help wherever he could. He was an interior decorator, and over and over again he helped beautify Zion.

Dr. Leonard W. Heroo loyally dedicated years of choice ministry as a teacher and preacher at Zion. He was a graduate of the Tutorial High School, Coinbra University, Portugal, a 1936 graduate of Zion Bible Institute, a 1939 graduate of the McKinley-Roosevelt University, Chicago, and he attended

Brown University from 1944 to 1946. He received numerous honorary degrees.

Miss Mary Campbell used her talent faithfully in the service of the school.

Mrs. Rosemary (MacDonald) Messerlian was very interested in children's work. Her training during their early years helped them, when they became parents themselves, train their own children in the nurture and admonition of the Lord. She also was involved in directing the practical work at Zion. She went to be with the Lord on December 11, 1981. Her winning smile and her love for people and Zion will ever be remembered by the school, the church, the Sunday school, and a host of friends.

After her death, many of her duties were assumed by Miss Libby Gomes who has given her life entirely to the work of Zion. One might say that her name, "Sister Libby," is heard more often on campus than any other name. We are blessed to have such an able and willing handmaiden as Sister Libby to oversee the practical duties on campus and to graciously act as Zion's official hostess.

Zion is very proud of her faculty, and it would be difficult to enumerate all of the teachers who have given their services, or to arrange them chronologically. God brought each one along for His own purposes, just when the school needed him/her the most, and used each one for His own glory.

At one time, Dr. Charles G. E. Chilton came as a friend and teacher of Homiletics. Some of us remember going to his class with fear and trembling and leaving, thinking that we could never make it, but most did! Rev. Irving Hoff came weekly from Harrisville, Rhode Island, to give studies in Prophecy. Miss Myra Beers taught several subjects. Miss Harriet Jones, an efficient teacher and registered nurse, taught subjects that were newly introduced into the curriculum. Rev. Arnold Waring filled a need on the teaching staff and ministered in the church. Rev. Swan Messerlian, a converted lawyer, filled a large place in giving legal advice for the school as well as being on the teaching staff. Louise Twist (now Louise Church) from Bangor, Maine, taught Dispensational Truth, and substituted in other subjects for several years. Esther Rollins, also from the Bangor area, helped in many ways. She worked in the office, handled the school paper, served as housemother, and teacher, having retired in the spring of 1992 when she turned eighty-one years of age.

Finally, crowning the staff, Sister Gibson, Zion's beloved leader, taught for many years, her main subject being Theology. She was not only a teacher, but she was a mother and a friend to all. Her exemplary Christian character left a deep impression upon all who knew her.

A new problem arose in 1941 that necessitated the incorporating of the Institute. Students coming in from Canada and other foreign countries were having great difficulty procuring leave to stay the nine months needed for the school year. On April 16, 1941, Zion Bible Institute was incorporated with the Rev. Christine A. Gibson as president. The school became officially recognized by the government of the United States as well as by the State of Rhode Island. Students coming from other countries then found it much easier to enroll.

The enrollment of the school year of 1941-42 numbered 100. It is with rejoicing that we say, as the number of students and workers increased, the Lord was ever faithful and sufficient. Zion faced soaring prices for food, heavy bills on coal, gas, electricity, insurance, and telephone. The record is this: God met every need as the Zion family continued to trust Him over and over again. Many times there was fasting and waiting on Him by all, and they were reminded time and time again "that

His eye is upon Zion, that He loves it, and that He will accomplish the work of His hands."

On December 7, 1941, Pearl Harbor Day, the United States went to war. It was a sad Sunday when we came home from the church service, flicked on the radio, and heard President Franklin D. Roosevelt announcing that war had been declared against the country of Japan. Many of Zion's young men went into active service during this time.

Several times when the Zion body met together, God indicated that He wanted her to enlarge her borders. In January of 1945, He spoke through the Spirit that He would do a new thing. On June 25 of that year, papers were signed for the purchase of adjoining property on Broadway. It was comprised of four buildings and land, and it was purchased for the sum of $25,000.00. To those who are living now and dealing in real estate, $25,000.00 for such a large amount of property seems almost laughable. At that time, however, to those at Zion's faith work, it was a stupendous sum. God indicated strongly that the houses and land should be purchased. It was a tremendous step of faith, but Sister Gibson assured the Zion family that nothing is impossible with God and the property was added to Zion's holdings. Out of small beginnings, God added to Zion — at the appointed time — that which was needed.

Chapter 19
The Operation of Faith

"Now abideth faith, hope, love, these three; but the greatest of these is love"

(1 Cor. 13:13).

"But faith which worketh by love"

(Gal. 5:6b).

Perhaps one of the most outstanding, if not *the* most outstanding characteristic of the founder of Zion, the Rev. Christine A. Gibson, was her expressive love for everyone with whom she came in contact. The one thing that people remember about her the most, strangely enough, is not her faith, but her love.

It almost seems, looking back, that faith followed naturally in her sincere life of love for all people. This love, concern, compassion, and interest in others bred togetherness in the work that made no sacrifice, monetary or personal, too great for one to give. Her example developed sacrifice in others. Hers was a wholesome, spiritual naturalness. She was simply a yielded child of God, appointed by His Spirit. There was no "put-on," no "show-off" position of accomplishment, no fancy appearance — just simply a loving soul with God's blessing on her life.

It was this simplicity, this naturalness, that attracted people to her. She was reachable at all times. The greatest preacher or the lowliest student could go to her and always find an audience. She was always ready to offer all that she had to others. Many times she would part with her last cent when someone had a need. When a room or a bed was needed, and none was available, she offered hers. She lived always for others.

At one time she needed a new spring coat, as hers was very shabby. A friend, seeing her worn-out coat, gave her enough money to purchase a new one. Just about that time, a tremendous need arose, and as usual, the school was called together to participate in sacrificing and giving. Sister Gibson said, "I will be the first to give. I had money given to me by a friend to purchase a new spring coat, but I give it to the Lord. We need it now." This happened three times, and finally the lady said, "I want to give you a spring coat! I will give you the money this time, but if you don't buy the coat, I am through!" The Spirit seemed to whisper to Sister Gibson, *"Go and buy yourself a new spring coat,"* and this time she did it.

Coupled with her love so evident to all, were humility and spirituality. She was always aware of the fact that she was only an "insignificant woman," but she loved God and His work, and the ministry of the Holy Spirit. She knew that these were the keys to getting things from God. Her dynamic ministry was not the result of formal training, or even natural ability, but a ministry of the Holy Spirit through a yielded life. Everything she did had to be done through the Word. If she didn't get a word from the Lord, she wouldn't move an inch in any direction — whether it was to buy a piece of land, build a building, or go somewhere to preach.

Sister Gibson had to be completely led of God — this she knew. This was made clear over and over again in every move made for an enlargement of the work at Zion. The Zion family was called to a time of fasting and prayer whenever there was an important decision to be made. *Life at Zion was a life of the Spirit.* No move was to be made in the wisdom of men. Guidance and leading were to come through the Word and the ministry of the Holy Spirit. How well we remember the times in prayer, finding God's will for the addition of a third story to the children's home and for the purchasing of the adjoining Goff property on Broadway.

God also gave a definite word regarding a new temple for Zion. Time and time again, Brother Wilbert Rich, Sister Gibson's brother-in-law (a very shy and quiet man), gave messages in tongues and was moved by the Holy Spirit to point to the land across the street from the tabernacle. The interpretation of the tongues was always that there would be a church on the vacant land which, up to this time, had been impossible to purchase. The owners had no inclination whatsoever to sell it to Zion. Whenever Sister Gibson called on the gentleman at his home regarding purchasing it, he always said, "No, I will never sell the property to Zion."

In actuality, the land did not look very inviting. It was overgrown with weeds, was never properly tended to by the owner, and had a broken, rickety, picket fence which surrounded it. It definitely was an eyesore, and yet, every once in a while, Brother Rich would be moved of God to point out the window to the weed patch and indicate that a church would be built there.

God's timing is different than ours, and the Zion family wondered when this would come to pass. The school was growing, the church was growing, more room was needed, and all involved felt that this piece of property should belong to Zion.

One day Rev. and Mrs. Jack Saunders, evangelists from Canada, visited Zion. He was a fine preacher and she had a beautiful singing voice. In one of the church services Sister Saunders rose to sing a solo. She began to sing, and suddenly we realized that she was not singing in English. She made the same journey to the same window that Uncle Bert had frequented with his message from God. Sister Saunders had never seen him do this, and she knew absolutely nothing about the planning for this piece of ground. However, she pointed to the same land, sang in the Spirit, and then gave the interpretation, singing in English. Her words were practically identical to those we had heard so often from Brother Rich. It was a confirmation that the blessed Holy Spirit gave — we were to keep this vision in our hearts and though it tarry, we should wait for it. Beyond this, Sister Saunders added one extra prophetic utterance, "Before the church building goes up on that property, a tent will be pitched there, so that summer outdoor meetings may be held."

One day the doorbell rang at Faith Home, and when the door was opened, there stood Charles Frankland, the owner of the property across from the tabernacle. He asked for Rev. Christine Gibson, was invited in, and he told her that he was now ready to sell the property for a certain sum. She praised the Lord and the property was purchased.

That summer a tent was pitched, children's meetings and evening services were held, and later on, there was a groundbreaking ceremony and a fall convention. Zion was getting ready to build a new church. True prophetic utterances always come to pass in God's time.

There was a sense of belonging to God and belonging to Zion. A beautiful spirit prevailed at Zion that captivated lives until they were eager to serve by the giving of their own lives. Remuneration was never considered. *Zion was not a place to get — it was a place to give.*

The deep understanding of God's dealings in Sister Gibson's life made her ministry one of leading others into surrender and consecration that called for a crucified life. She constantly insisted that no one should even think of associating himself with the work of Zion unless he was sure that God had called him, and was ready for crucifixion of the carnal nature.

How well we recall the heart-searching times when we were prostrated before God under her straightforward Bible teaching, when she pointed out the need for carnal lives and minds to be placed on the altar, where God could burn out selfishness and pride. Morning prayers turned into hours of intercession and surrender. Many times classes did not convene for days. The spiritual was more important than the intellectual during these times of consecration to God.

Sister Gibson was a prime example for the students to follow, in fulfilling the divine commission. In 1947, *The Fellowship Field* carried her article on this very theme:

> "Jesus of Nazareth, a prophet mighty in deed and word before God and all the people," who, through the Holy Ghost, first taught by word and then by example, continues to teach and work miracles through His children today. He was the first great Teacher, the "kernel of wheat" fallen into the ground from which was to spring up the greatest miracle of the age, the Christian Church.
>
> The Church of Christ is built up — not on the memory of a dead Christ, a crucifix, or a cross — but on the Risen Savior who left behind Him the power of an endless life, power to transform sinful men into holy men, power to be an overcomer on a daily basis, and power to remove selfishness and every evil thing that casts down and hinders.
>
> The Divine Commission, with the promise, "Ye shall receive power, after the Holy Ghost is come upon you," was not given to men of rank or great

learning or wealth, but to a few chosen disciples who were to go forth and teach the things that He taught. Christ unfolded to them things pertaining to the Kingdom of God. *"My kingdom,"* He said, *"is not of this world."* Some of the things He taught were hard to be understood, but to His disciples, He promised the "Spirit of Truth" to guide them into all truth, and to show them things to come. These disciples were not only taught, but commanded by Him, to wait for the "promise of the Father," — the enduement of power from on high. We have the record that they continued in prayer and supplication until the Day of Pentecost was fully come, and the Holy Ghost was poured out upon them. Thus equipped, they carried out His command, *"Go ye into all the world and preach the Gospel to every creature."* These signs shall follow believers — "In my name shall they cast out devils, they shall speak with new tongues, they shall lay hands on the sick and they shall recover."

Upon similar lines and principles, our work here in Zion, including both our Bible school and Evangelistic Fellowship, has been built. Some of our students, baptized with the Holy Ghost, have gone forth into foreign lands, as well as the homeland, fulfilling the divine commission, the Lord working with them, confirming the Word with signs following. Sinful men are transformed into saints, sick bodies are healed, evil spirits cast out, and children are converted and baptized with the Holy Spirit.

Throughout the years, hundreds of young men and women have entered our doors to learn lessons in the life of faith. The three-year course which we offer, gives them more than a head knowledge. They experience and understand the practical side of faith. Many are the testimonies given, that they learned the first steps of faith by trusting God for a three-cent stamp, a tube of toothpaste, or a bar of soap. Students who graduate from our school are instructed not to seek easy places with good salaries, but to go forth as the early disciples did, relying upon God for their support.

Speaking from a personal viewpoint, I can say that in all the years of our trust in God for thousands of dollars to buy food and pay bills of every description, He has never failed us. He has kept us steadfast through dark days of sorrow, weakness, loneliness, and trial. His presence has never left us.

Students of all nationalities find an open door at Zion Bible Institute, for God is no respecter of persons, and the divine commission is, "Teach all nations."

Years ago, in the early days of the work, God spoke to us that Zion would be "beautiful for situation, the joy of the whole earth," and we are now realizing the fulfillment of that prophecy, through our Bible school and Zion Evangelistic Fellowship. Our workers are truly bringing joy to darkened lives as they go to different parts of the earth and preach the Gospel.

We desire every friend who reads this article to take Zion Bible Institute, students and faculty alike, upon your hearts and pray daily for us. Pray for these young consecrated students who feel the urge to go forward. Many of them have left all to follow Jesus. They have dedicated their lives to His service, having neither silver nor gold to give, but giving what is of greater worth — lives to lay at His feet.

This theme continued throughout experiences and victories that formed the spiritual side of the family at Zion. We were developing into a body of overcoming Christians that took the divine commission seriously.

In reality, this closeness of purpose, life, and ministry welded a family of Zion that even today cannot be understood by many. Sharing burdens, needs, and victories — yes, even defeats — brings people together, and this togetherness could be seen and felt. In its truest sense, this bond is not physical or geographical, but a spiritual unity. It seems to follow, like day after night, that this kind of atmosphere of love and unity produces a climate that sets the stage for faith to operate. No mountain looked too high to climb and no ocean looked too wide to cross. God has been so big in Zion's life and work that nothing seemed impossible with Him. The Ebenezers of yesterday taught that the Egyptians and Philistines couldn't stand before ancient Israel, and they can't stand before Zion today.

This was the life and ministry of our beloved founder, the Rev. Christine A. Gibson. Her humility, love, and yieldedness to the guidance and control of the Holy Spirit gave all an example and an inspiration that still lives in hearts today. In a day of shallow religious experiences, the emphasis often being placed on the material rather than the spiritual, it is important to the following generations that we as Christians keep constantly before us the truths and patterns of life that gave us what we have today.

Zion was not designed on a drawing board at executive board meetings. It came through vision, revelation, sacrifice, suffering, obedience, and God's mighty presence in the lives of those who have gone on before, and others who are still living today.

After having bought the new property where Zion Gospel Temple stands today, it was suggested that a second story be added to one of the old buildings. It seemed the natural thing to do, and after talking it over, Sister Gibson gave permission to move ahead with the endeavor. Brother William Gundersen, who was in the work at Zion with his wife, Virginia, oversaw this project. New lumber was purchased, materials were brought in, the sound of striking hammers reached our ears, and we heard saws buzzing away. Suddenly Sister Gibson received a call from the City Hall, saying that the neighbors had passed around a petition, asking that work on the addition cease immediately. Neighbors contended that an addition would bring darkness into portions of their homes, and it would block their views; therefore, they had enough names on a petition to stop the work. Some folks who wanted the addition, said, "Well, we don't have to pay any attention to that! The town just showed us the petition, but they did not issue a command saying not to build."

Sister Gibson went to prayer as she did about everything. As she was praying about the situation, God spoke to her and said, *"Love worketh no ill to its neighbor, therefore love is the fulfilling of the law"* (Rom. 13:10). She rose from her knees, went to the back of Faith Home, looked over to where the men were very busy on the building and called to them. They could not hear her because of all the noise. She then went down a short flight of stairs and walked over toward them. When they noticed her, Brother Gundersen came down from the roof to greet her and she said, "Bill, I want your men to tear down the second-floor addition."

"What do you mean? he asked.

"The Lord has shown me that we are not to build that second floor," she answered.

Respecting her wishes, and being assured that God had spoken to her, Brother Gundersen had the work stopped, took down the lumber, and there was no second floor added — much to the delight of the neighbors.

This was definitely a word from the Lord, because not too long after that, Zion received notification from the State of Rhode Island that many of Zion's buildings were going to either have to be razed or be taken to another location, since a new road was going to be built. It would be a wider road and a highway tunnel was going from south to north underneath Broadway. They would be buying up some of Zion's land; therefore, the second floor on that building would have been of no avail. How good to know that God is in control! He knows about the future even when we do not.

The quickening power of the Holy Spirit changed a frail, ordinary woman into a mighty warrior in the army of the Lord. She humbly recognized, along with St. Paul, the truth that she possessed neither fancy speech nor wisdom, but that she knew simply Christ crucified. She realized that in her fearfulness and trembling, she could approach the tasks she was called to, in the demonstration and power of the Spirit. Paul said, in First Corinthians, that this was so that our faith should not stand in the wisdom of men, but in the power of God.

Let us now take a brief look at her pulpit ministry — a ministry as dynamic and forceful as any man has ever possessed. It was dynamic because of the Spirit's control over it, and forceful because she was a devoted student of the Word. She had a fresh revelation of His Word as He dealt with her daily in the burdens, cares, struggles, and victories of the work at Zion. She always considered the staff and church members, along with the students, to be her family. Problems there were everyone's problems; consequently, everyone in the church became part of Zion. Burdens, visions, needs — all were shared together. It was one big family, standing together in the hour of need and rejoicing together in the hour of triumph.

Can we ever forget those times of revelation? Hundreds of times our sister rose from her seat under the anointing and thrilled our souls with God's word as He poured it through her in a brand-new quickening for the occasion. Can we forget her ministry of prophecy, tongues and interpretations? Can we forget her exposition of the Bible that came through the heart-rending experiences of her own life? Can we forget her open arms for every man, woman, and child? Can we forget the undaunted faith, the unfeigned love, the deep understanding of her human side, and her compassion that let her feel every person's need as if it were her own? No! We cannot forget, and we must not forget!

Chapter 20
Through Faith They Obtained

> "Let us hold fast the profession of our faith without wavering, (for He is faithful that promised)"
> (Heb. 10:23).

In the early 1940s, after a celebrated burning of the mortgage on the Zion property was held, God made it very plain that greater things were in store for His work there. As already stated, the Goff property was purchased, consisting of four houses and large lots of land on Broadway in East Providence, adjacent to Faith Home. It was a parcel deal — it could not be broken up to be purchased by sections. The buyer had to take all or nothing. Stunned by such an offer, and relieved after the final payments on the long-time mortgage, Sister Gibson went to prayer. God directed her to bring the proposition before the people of the church. It was clearly indicated by the Holy Spirit that this was in God's plan for Zion, and again, the Spirit impressed the Zion family to lengthen her cords and to strengthen her stakes (see Isaiah 54:2). Thus, a new step of faith was taken.

The real-estate holdings of Ralph E. Goff which adjoined the grounds of Faith Home passed into the hands of Zion Bible Institute, Inc. The agreement transferred more than 22,000 square feet of land and four buildings. Mr. Goff, while signing the documents closing the deal, declared, "Two weeks ago I never dreamed that I'd be selling all this property, and I really don't know why I'm selling it now. I've always been satisfied with my tenants, and I get good income from my investments." Unbeknownst to Mr. Goff, God was using him as one more thread in the pattern He was weaving for Zion.

Rev. Christine A. Gibson, president of Zion Bible Institute, signed the papers on behalf of the school and declared, "God is moving in Zion and doing a new thing. Surely, Zion is pulling up her stakes and lengthening her cords, in accordance with the great plan and purpose of our God."

God moved on the people to give what they had, and spontaneously, bank accounts were emptied, checks written, monies brought to God, and pledges made and kept. The Bible school students, inspired by the Holy Ghost to give to the expansion program, rolled up cash and pledges totalling more than $4,500.00. The church also caught the vision of sharing the blessing, and boosted the total cash and pledges to $8,500.00, with four businessmen alone donating $2,000.00. The entire amount was raised within forty-eight hours. All this was in answer to a step of faith; thus, the Goff property was purchased.

This was followed by a terrific explosion in school enrollment and God was on the move — never too late. World War II was over and floods of young people were looking to Zion for ministry training.

A new children's home was established at 838 Broadway, under the direction of Rev. and Mrs. Henry Sinclair.

The tabernacle was inadequate, and men reasoned how good it would be to have a church on Broadway. In the area between Faith Home and the newly purchased buildings, a large sign was erected in the middle of the land. It read, "This is the proposed site of the new Zion Gospel Temple."

However, God had another place, and through a mighty demonstration, the Holy Ghost confirmed the original place, the same that had been indicated earlier by His servant, Brother

Rich, and by his handmaiden, Sister Saunders. God's place for the new church was not on Broadway, but on the corner of Gurney Street and Leonard Avenue. This was indicated over and over again: First there would be a tent and then a temple, all for God's glory. God said the temple would be built in troublesome times and the people of God upheld the vision. Thus, man's plans were brought in line with God's design for Zion.

One day there came to Sister Gibson a mighty vision from heaven. She saw Broadway, but said that it was not Broadway as it was then. The new Broadway was wide and stately, and on Zion's front property, an administration building stood. The Goff houses were gone in the vision and when Sister Gibson shared the vision, joy and assurance filled the hearts of the people. It came to pass just as God had shown His handmaiden. The state took the Goff buildings and made Broadway a four-lane highway, with a good-sized median. The Christine A. Gibson Memorial Administration Building was erected on Broadway after her death and dedicated to God. His glory came, as promised, and filled the house.

The building of the temple began when Sister Gibson turned over the first shovelful of dirt on the corner lot on August 15, 1948. What a glorious day when the temple was completed! It was the temple that was long ago prophesied by men and women of God. The work on the temple was under the direction of Rev. William Gundersen. Others were specifically called to Zion for the time, and saw the vision become reality.

People were again moved upon to give money so that God's work would go forward. Men, women, young people, and children all gave, to bring the vision to fruition. The people had a mind to work, and talent and labor were dedicated to the building of the temple. Sacrificial offerings were laid upon the altar of God without coercion. People gave watches, rings, jewelry, autos, property, gifts — great and small — at God's altar and the temple went up. Never in Zion's history had a people totally emptied their pockets so willingly and cheerfully. The news of it spread throughout the country, and alumni and friends came to the help of God; thus, the temple was completed.

Before the finishing of the interior, the glory of the Lord came down, and for days the Lord moved mightily upon His people. Never will any of us forget the revival of January, 1952. Young and old, ministers and deacons, sinners and saints sought God. As the Spirit hovered over like a cloud, a mighty revival swept through the people. There were healings, and gifts, and calls to salvation. There were mighty deliverances as God poured out His blessing upon His people. The meals were often overlooked or forgotten. The clock's hours held little importance, for God came down in the midst and His glory filled the temple.

Zion Gospel Temple was dedicated on March 19, 1952. Through an unctionized ministry in the Spirit, Sister Gibson, as a handmaiden of the Lord, was ordained of God to minister in the temple from the altar of God. It was promised that the people would see the light of the Lord of Hosts, and that His glory would fill His house and all that stood therein. Thus, Rev. Christine A. Gibson, woman of faith, ministered a few years in the temple before God called her higher.

The revelation of truth that Sister Gibson shared with the people was inspiring and challenging. Who could forget her sermons, "Saviors or Judges?" from the book of Obadiah [See Appendix A], or "The Called-out Company" from the parable of the ten virgins, or "Because of Her Importunity" from the parable of the unjust judge, or "Digging Ditches" from the book of Second Kings? They truly are numbered among the classics.

Chapter 21
The Alpha and Omega

"Looking unto Jesus, the Author and Finisher of our faith"
(Heb. 12:2).

On the land adjoining the area at the rear of the temple, on the corner of Cole Street and Leonard Avenue, sat a big, old and sprawling shack bulging with iron, metal, wood, and junk. It belonged to a junk dealer and it was an eyesore, especially because it sat so close to such a beautiful temple. The owner had no desire to release this property, but God had another plan. In a most remarkable way, this parcel of land was offered to Zion, and was immediately purchased. This provided a spacious parking lot for the temple, all to the glory of God. The Lord can cause even the wrath of the unbelievers to bring glory to His name.

A very worn-out and run-down cottage sat empty on land adjoining the temple on Gurney Street and was a detriment to the environment and to the beauty of the area, as well. Zion needed and wanted the property, but the owners had no desire at all to sell it. Again, God intervened, and in a matter of a few days the property was in the name of Zion Bible Institute. The cottage was repaired and was used to house young men for one year. It was jokingly referred to as the "Cram-in Cottage." A lovely parking area was later landscaped there for Zion's use. This was also but a light thing in the sight of the Lord. (See 2 Kings 3:18.)

As God had promised, Sister Gibson stood behind the sacred desk in the temple, ministering to the people for a few years. They were years of victory and years of glory. Many came into the house of God and received wonderful touches from heaven. Outstanding Holy Ghost-anointed cantatas and conventions, graduations and baccalaureates, all-nation rally days, and services marked the early days of the temple as the Holy Spirit manifested himself over and over to the glory of God. Many have come in and gone out of Zion's portals to share the message of salvation and deliverance, healing and victory, with people of every continent on this globe.

The local radio ministry of Zion Bible Institute began in 1938 from radio station WSAR in Fall River, Massachusetts. Rev. Leonard W. Heroo was the radio preacher and Rev. Edward B. Hill, the announcer. In the early 1930s, groups from Zion traveled to Wellesley to broadcast the Gospel over station WBSO. Between 1939 and 1953, the Institute produced broadcasts from time to time as opportunities came and radio station time was available.

In 1953 the radio department of Zion was founded on a permanent basis by the Rev. Edward B. Hill. Beginning in the spring of 1954, "Temple Time" was broadcast continuously on Sunday mornings and also daily, for many years. The beginning of this radio ministry saw Rev. Hill broadcasting from the basement of a dormitory at Zion Bible Institute. Through the years of progress, "Temple Time" was broadcast from several locations on Zion's campus.

In 1960, Rev. Hill founded the Christian Broadcasting Association with the following serving as officers of his corporation: Rev. Edward B. Hill, president and treasurer; Mr. Walter Rodrigues, vice-president; and Mrs. Sylvia Hill, secretary.

The three years following the dedication of the temple were glorious years for Zion and for Sister Gibson. We have already covered some of the events that took place during this period. She continued to lead the work, to plan and to move ahead in faith — until the very end.

However, the days of Rev. Christine A. Gibson's sojourn here were drawing to a close. Suddenly, in the midst of the very busy month of May, our beloved Mother Gibson was stricken ill. The seniors were preparing for graduation, but Sister Gibson was preparing to march on to her eternal reward. In fact, throughout the year of 1955, those close to Sister Gibson noticed a weakness in her body and that an occasional terrific pain would pass through her head. We ministered to her and cared for her during these periods of pain, and in a day or so, she always seemed to be better. She experienced many divine healings in her life of faith, and often when brought low by sickness and despair, the word of faith would come to her, and she would rise up in Jesus' name and overcome. But this was different. The servant of God knew that she was going Home. A deep peace settled over her and she waited.

Mrs. Ilda Finger, a very close friend and associate of the work in Zion, and also a sister of Dr. Leonard Heroo, arrived from New York. She was a registered nurse with many demands for her time in New York, but as once promised, she came and gave the best of care to Sister Gibson. Sister Gibson requested that she not be sent to a hospital and the specialist who came to Faith Home asked that we put her in a hospital bed and have a competent nurse care for her. This would give her the privilege of remaining in her own home during her illness. The specialist returned to doctor her from time to time. The Zion family prayed long and often. Convention time came and a speaker system was set up in her room so that she could hear the sermons. Rev. Benjamin Crandall preached the baccalaureate that year, and she was able to hear his message and other sermons throughout the convention days.

I remember an experience of my own when I went into her room on the afternoon of May 29 and talked with her. She said to me, "Mamie, I have not really looked through the class book. Would you come by the bed and turn the pages? Also, bring me my glasses."

I did this, and we went through every page of the *Zionian.* We cried some and laughed some. She seemed so vibrant and I felt good in my soul. I thought, "I don't believe she will die." As I left the room, she said, "Be sure and come in after the evening service, and tell me all about it."

That evening, as we were sitting in church, Sunday, May 29, 1955, at the age of seventy-six, our faithful leader heard her final command, *"Come up higher."* Sylvia Hill, her niece, was passing by the door of Faith Home and was told that Sister Gibson had died. She rushed over to the church and made the announcement. For a moment, it was hard to believe. Sister Gibson left us with the challenge of her faith. The memory of her total consecration to God and His work shall ever live in the hearts of all whose lives she touched. Strong men and little children wept sorely at the news of her passing. Everyone felt that they had lost a good, good friend. We cried aloud together.

That night no one went to bed. The streets were filled with people, and passing cars were wondering, "What is going on in that place?" Some stopped to inquire. The next day had been set for graduation exercises for the class of 1955. Zion's administration met and decided it would be Sister Gibson's desire to have the class go through with the graduation exercises as planned.

As the graduating class marched down the aisle to receive diplomas, each graduate had a never-to-be-forgotten sense of love and an inspired awareness of responsibility to live the life of faith and do the work of God. A beautiful vigil was kept in loving memory of Sister Gibson. The presence of God filled the temple day and night. Friends came from near and far to pay their last respects to our Mother in Israel. The memorial service was sad, but the light of the word of faith shone through the tears, and hearts were encouraged to press on in Him. Although God had taken His handmaiden, His work at Zion would go on.

The days that followed were difficult, and the loss of our friend and leader was deeply felt. However, the God of all comfort comforted His people. The weeks and months of adjustment were hard, and at times it seemed as though the old ship Zion would be overwhelmed by the waves of questioning, doubt, and fears. But God, through His Word, directed that in love and understanding, His work was to go on.

The good ship Zion sails on victoriously today, still with Christine's God at the helm, guiding, leading, and directing — mile after mile after mile. What a living memorial to a great woman of faith — Zion, the joy of the whole earth!

Appendix A

Appendix A

Sermon Extract
"Saviors or Judges?"
by
Rev. Christine A. Gibson

"Saviors or judges: which class are you in?" This question was asked me by the Holy Spirit as I knelt by the side of a chair in the sitting room of our cottage, Eden Rest, at Old Orchard, Maine, where I recently had gone for a much-needed rest.

It came to me as a heart-searching question and greatly arrested my attention, bringing a flood-tide of thoughts to my mind. Saviors? Judges? I knew the Scriptures had much to say on this subject. I got my Bible and refreshed my mind by looking up several passages, for I remembered that several years ago, God gave me a message on "Saviors," and I felt that perhaps I was about to receive added light on this wonderful subject.

As I searched the Bible, I received such light and blessing to my soul, that I was impelled to give the teaching I had received to those who gathered at Eden Rest the following Sunday afternoon. The Holy Spirit sealed it as the message for the hour. Those who were present seemed greatly moved by it and expressed their desire to have it given to other congregations. With this in view, I am sending it forth in this issue of *Faith*, believing that it will reach those whom I am unable to personally visit.

The first passage of Scripture given to me was Romans 8:34, "Who is he that condemneth? [does the work of a judge]. It is Christ that died, yea rather, that is risen again, who is even at the right hand of God, who also maketh intercession for us." I saw at once that He (the Christ), the only One who had the legal right to condemn or judge us, had become our Savior. Instead of condemning us, He is sitting at the right hand of God as our Intercessor, praying and pleading our case, as stated in another passage, "We have an Advocate [lawyer] with the Father, Jesus Christ the righteous" (1 John 2:1).

O, how this thought overwhelmed me: If He, the only One who was justified in passing judgment upon the human race, refused to do so in this Gospel age (as is recorded in John 8:15-16, when He said to the Pharisees, "Ye judge after the flesh; I judge no man. And yet if I judge, my judgment is true"), how dare we poor, finite human beings sit in fleshly judgment on any of our brethren? I paused a moment before looking up other references, and my heart cried out, "O God, I would be in the class with saviors, and not among judges!"

Let us not bring judgment upon ourselves by judging others, as Jesus shows us in Matthew 7:2, "For with what judgment ye judge, ye shall be judged; and with what measure ye mete, it shall be measured to you again."

O, may this not be the reason for the dearth of spiritual power in many of our assemblies today? Brethren, are we judging each other after the flesh, instead of loving and praying for one another? Let us not forget Paul's admonition to the Galatians (5:13-15): "Brethren, ye have been called unto liberty; only use not liberty for an occasion to the flesh, but by love serve one another. For all the law is fulfilled in one word, even in this; Thou shalt love thy neighbor as thyself. But if ye bite and devour one another, take heed that ye be not consumed one of another." See also James 4:11,12, "Speak not evil one of another, brethren. He that speaketh evil of his brother, and judgeth his brother, speaketh evil of the law, and judgeth the law: but if thou judge the law, thou art not a doer of the law, but a judge. There is one lawgiver, who is able to save and to destroy: who art thou that judgest another?"

Yes, friend, there is one Lawgiver, able to save and to destroy, and He refuses to hand over the position to any other. Let us not, therefore, treat the Law with contempt and thus bring judgment on ourselves by so doing. Christ is ordained of God to be Judge (See Acts 10:42), but the time is yet in the future. In this day, He is our Great High Priest, who ever lives to make intercession for us (Heb. 7:25). Shall we not, therefore, stand with Him, and be among the saviors who are coming up on Mount Zion, God's place of "perfected beauty," as recorded in Obadiah 21, and help carry on the marvelous ministry He began on this earth?

This is, I believe, the purpose of the outpoured Spirit: To call out a company of overcomers, as saviors, and prepare them for future rulership with the One who is coming back to sit on His throne, as King of kings and Lord of lords, the Judge of the whole earth!

What is the ministry of a savior? Several Scriptures were given me as the answer.

The first type of a savior was Moses, in his intercession for Israel. This was the group that was so unthankful to him, and at whose hand he suffered much when the opportunity arose for him to be the head of another nation. They failed God, in making and worshipping a golden calf. God would have brought judgment upon them by consuming them, but Moses stepped into the gap and became their intercessor. "And Moses returned unto the Lord, and said, O, this people have sinned a great sin, and have made them gods of gold. Yet now, if Thou wilt forgive their sin —; and if not, blot me, I pray Thee, out of thy book which thou has written'' (Exod. 32:31,32).

Thus, Moses saved the whole nation. Are we willing to stand in the gap and pray for our brethren who despitefully use us? That is the ministry of a savior.

The second type of a savior is Joseph, giving bread to his brethren who had sold him to a company of Ishmaelites and caused him to suffer wrongfully. He became their savior. Listen to his words, "God sent me before you to preserve you a posterity in the earth, and to save your lives by a great deliverance. So now it was not you that sent me hither, but God" (Gen. 45:7,8).

Yes, he was a savior and was used of God as a bread-giver. O friends, let us go through the testing times and become "bread" for our brethren. Out of our experiences at the hands of loved ones, we shall be enabled to feed them with the Bread of Life. Joseph was but a shadow of our true Joseph (Jesus), who gave His flesh for the life of the world, and even for those who consented to His death. Each one was in line to reap the benefits of Calvary. Yes, only those who are willing to go through the gates and suffer with Him, are able to give "strong meat" (corn) to the brethren (see Ps. 105:17-22).

Daniel, in his intercession for his people, also gives us insight into the ministry of saviors: He takes their place and prays as though he were a sinner, "We have sinned, and have committed iniquity, and have done wickedly, and have rebelled, even by departing from thy precepts and from thy judgments" (Dan. 9:5).

Read the whole prayer and you will see that he has taken the sinner's place and numbers himself with the transgressors, although he is a righteous man, greatly beloved of God (cf. Isa. 53:12). This is the ministry of saviors — to let the reproach of others fall on them, and to be numbered with transgressors, looking like one, although, like their Master, blameless.

Are we willing for such a ministry? Of course, we shall be misjudged and misunderstood as He was, but what of it? O, what a joy to know that we have stood with others, full of infirmities and weaknesses of the flesh, and have allowed their reproach to fall upon us, not pleasing ourselves, but living for others, as it is written of Christ, "The reproaches of them that reproached thee fell on me" (Rom. 15:3).

What a joy, too, to know that we have prayed them through to glory, and, in that day, we will be crowned with rejoicing as we behold them, standing with us in His presence. This will compensate for the heartaches we experienced while going through trying times, with and for them. Jesus, "for the joy that was set before him endured the cross, despising the shame, and is set down at the right hand of the throne of God" (Heb. 12:2). Let us also despise the shame of this ministry and endure the cross, and we, in time, will also sit with Him as His associate rulers in His future kingdom.

Saviors or judges — which will it be? I say, by all means, let us be saviors. Let us go as good Samaritans to every poor soul who has fallen by the wayside, and bind up wounds, pouring in oil and wine. Let us not go as Pharisaical priests and Levites who had nothing to offer others but censure and condemnation, taking the other side of the road. Let us not think that we are so holy that we cannot contaminate our persons with others, and be bent on saving our own lives while others are perishing. God forbid that we should be among that number!

Let us, therefore, obey the call, and go forth unto Him, our blessed Savior, without the camp, bearing His reproach.

APPENDIX B

Appendix B

Sermon
"Signs of the Times"
(The European War in the Light of Prophecy)
[Delivered in 1914]
by
Rev. Reuben A. Gibson

I was in the city of Bangor, Maine, the morning when Germany's ultimatum, challenging the world to war, appeared in the daily papers. That very morning, in a Bangor daily, an article was printed, written by H. Katz, principal of the Hebrew Institute of Bangor, calling attention to that day being a special fast day of the Jews, commemorating the siege of Jerusalem by Nebuchadnezzar, king of Babylon, about 2500 years ago. "The fast," the professor wrote, "is known by the name Tishah Be-Av, which falls this year [1914] on Saturday, August 1. But, as it is unlawful for the Jews to fast on Saturday, it will be held Sunday, August 2, to lament the loss of our country."

The proclamation of war, involving all the nations of the world, and the announcement of the celebration of a Jewish fast of a *political nature* appearing at the same time in the daily press, were to me most significant and thrilling. For, beyond, and above, all secondary causes of the war (i.e. empire building, the promotion of one nation's commerce over the other, the multiplying of its merchant marine forces, territorial grabbing, racial pride, and religious prejudices), the chief and primary cause is found in the Word of God, and known to every student of prophetic Scriptures. In the fewest words, the cause is this: The chronological closing of the times of the Gentiles, and the restoration of ancient Israel to national life and dominion.

What is meant by the *times of the Gentiles?* A cursory glance at the Word of God in the history of nations will show Israel as the *first selected nation* to hold governmental supremacy over the surrounding nations, beginning with David, king of Judah and Israel, and reaching its highest national glory in his son, Solomon's reign.

This is followed in the course of centuries, by Israel's national decline and fall, through disobedience to God, and the rise of the supremacy of the Gentile power of the ancient kingdom of Babylon. This period of time in history, which indicates at once the dispersion and punishment of the Jewish people, and the supremacy of the Gentiles, is known in the Scriptures as "the time of the Gentiles." It seems to have pleased God to have given his prophet, Daniel, 600 years before Christ, a clear prophetic outline of the course of the ages, beginning with the captivity of the Jews and the supremacy of the Gentile power of Babylon, down to the end of this present age.

In the second and seventh chapters of Daniel, there is a clear prediction of the course of the successive "world powers" which are to bear rule, down to the end. In the image of chapter two, the head of gold represents Babylonian power; the breast of silver represents the double kingdom which succeeded Babylon — the Medo-Persian empire; the body of brass, the Grecian empire, under Alexander and his successors; and the legs of iron represented the Roman Empire, divided into its eastern and western sections. After the legs of iron, we come to the feet and toes of the image. These are a mixture of iron and clay, partly strong and partly brittle. These may fitly describe the nations of Europe, which are the result of the breaking up of the Roman Empire over 1,000 years ago. The iron may represent the strength of Roman law, while the brittle clay may fitly represent the spirit of democracy, which has grown so manifestly in all the nations of the world during the past few decades.

The vision of Nebuchadnezzar in chapter two corresponds in its general features with the vision given the prophet in chapter seven. In the former case, the nations are seen as a colossal image, great and magnificent. In the case of God's prophet, he sees the nations as savage beasts, ready to devour one another. However, we should not fail to notice that even in the image, a steady deterioration from head to foot, from gold to mud, indicates God's view of this so-called "progress" of our civilization. The image had a poor foundation with its heaviest metal at the top.

The central point of both chapters, however, is the *second advent of Christ,* and the establishment of the Kingdom of God on earth. In chapter two, verse 44, we read, "In the days of these kings shall the God of heaven set up a kingdom which shall never be destroyed." We may ask, who are these kings represented by the ten horns of the fourth beast in chapter seven? They are ten kings who shall arise and shall be headed by one great ruler over them all, in a kind of international confederacy — one head, perhaps a "United States of Europe."

From this, it will be seen that we are living today in a time when great events of world-wide significance may be expected to transpire. Many Christians who accept the Bible as the inspired Word of God, believe that while we may not know "the day nor the hour" of Christ's return to earth, we are nearing the time indicated in the vision of the falling of "the stone" which strikes the feet of the image and becomes a great mountain which fills the earth.

Connected very closely with the "times of the Gentiles" in their course and succession of each other, bearing rule down to the end, with the overthrow of ten kingdoms (the last phase of Gentile rule), and the return of the Lord Jesus as Earth's Coming Ruler, is, as we have already stated, the dispersion and punishment of the Jewish people.

In Leviticus 26, it is repeated four times that "seven times" of punishment would pass over Israel for their sins. These "seven times" of Israel's punishment occur simultaneously with the times of the supremacy of the Gentiles. A "time" in Scripture often means a prophetic year, according to the Levitical calendar of 360 days, and again, prophetic days are often reckoned "a day for a year" (Numbers 14:34, Ezekiel 4:6). These "seven times" or seven years of 360 days would mean 2520 days, and a day for a year, would mean 2520 years. This is the divine measuring rod of the times of Israel's punishments and of the times of Gentile supremacy over the Holy Land.

From where shall we begin to reckon? Naturally, from the time of Israel's Babylonian captivity, about the year B.C. 605 or 606. This was the beginning of the dispersion of the Jews. Counting 2520 years from B.C. 605 or 606, we come to 1914 or 1915. To say the least, this, in the light of the present upheaval in Europe, is very interesting and significant. We do not claim more than approximate accuracy for the above dates, but God's clock of the ages will surely be correct and standard time.

We are not predicting the date of the second advent of Christ, nor the end of the world. We are merely pointing out that we are probably living in the beginning of the end of "the times of the Gentiles," and that we are approaching the end of the present dispensation.

It may be considered too early to begin to speak of possible results of this terrible war, but there seem to be certain facts which are apparent to all. The coming of Turkey into this war, adds materially to the subject from a prophetic standpoint.

Turkey is the Gentile power which has, in the language of the Scriptures, "trodden down" Jerusalem these many years. Jesus said, *"Jerusalem shall be trodden down of the Gentiles, until the times of the Gentiles be fulfilled"* (Luke 21:24). If the times of the Gentiles are about complete, we may surely look for the release of Jerusalem from Turkish rule.

Now the question is, in the event of Turkey relinquishing her claim on Palestine, to whom will the Holy Land revert? I think we may safely answer: to Abraham's seed who undoubtedly hold, by divine purpose, the title deeds to that land of promise. Already the Zionist Congress of the lovers of Palestine, are arranging a request for the Powers to recognize their national organization after the war is over. Furthermore, it ought not to be forgotten that the finances of Europe are largely in the control of the Jew, and if this war, in its last analysis, resolves itself into a question of finance, it is more than likely that the Jew may have a good deal to say, perhaps in a quiet way, as to the terms of peace.

Some are under the impression that this stupendous conflict now raging is the Battle of Armageddon. It is not Armageddon. The Scriptures are too plain concerning the nature, time, and place of that last deadly stand that the nations of earth will take, in the world's last war. The present struggle is between opposing world powers; Armageddon will be the united world powers in battle array against the Jews — by that time, restored to their own land — and against *the Son of God himself* who will then be accepted as their Messiah. Its storm center will be Palestine and the surrounding country, and Jerusalem, in particular. "Alas! for that day is great, so that none is like it: it is even the time of Jacob's (the Jews') trouble, but he shall be saved out of it" (Jer. 30:7).

Read part of the story of Armageddon in Zechariah 14. Read the whole chapter carefully, noting especially verses two, three, and four. See also Zechariah 12. Armageddon is the world's final conflict, when all earthly kingdoms will be brought to naught forever, by being suddenly smitten by "the stone" of Daniel (prophecy already noted). Read of this same smiting stone in the act of delivering the death blow in Revelation 19:11-21. Verses seventeen and eighteen there, together with Ezekiel 39:17-20, absolutely identify the scene as one and the same.

While we have not reached Armageddon yet, there can be little question that the present mad war is its forerunner, preparing the way. One thing is settled in the heavens, and recorded on earth: Earth's judgment day is close at hand. It has been on record for some 2500 years, and there are today, in millions of homes over the world, more copies of this Record than of any other writing extant. It behooves every one to search the Scriptures and see if these things are so. Part of this long, existing record is that the present dispensation is to close with a veritable *reign of terror,* beside which, the horrors of the French revolution, when the streets of Paris ran with blood, will sink into insignificance.

At the right moment, those whom God sees to be ready, will be caught away — the resurrected dead and the living ones — according to First Thess. 4:16,17. This will be followed immediately by the political rise of a man more brilliant, daring, and powerful, than any that the earth has ever seen — a man as truly inspired of Satan as Christ was inspired of God. He is the *anti-christ,* embodying in his own person, all the evil of all the evil men, systems, and powers, which, through the centuries, have been his types. He will soon have the poor, befooled world at his feet, and under color of being its long looked-for deliverer, he will lead it through rapidly increasing and ever-deepening horrors, to its doom. Having run his appalling career of seven years, he will be miraculously destroyed by the sudden appearance, in dazzling glory, of *the Man* who once before, presented himself to the world — *that* time, to be spit upon and nailed to a felon's cross; *this* time, to demolish all national governments, completely overturning the existing order of things, and setting up His own glorious *Kingdom on the Earth*. It will be this Jesus, the Son of God, the Savior of the world, King of kings, and Lord of all.

Then will come the closing scene in human history. It is Israel's deliverance. And it is more. It is the end of all wrong, greed, graft, crime, and misrule. It is God's answer to groaning creation. It is the coming of the King whose right it is to reign. Hallelujah! Hallelujah!

>All hail the power of Jesus' name!
>Let angels prostrate fall —
>Bring forth the royal diadem
>And crown Him Lord of all!
>
>(Selected)

R.A.G.
With extracts from R.A. Jaffray
in *Alliance Weekly* and
E. Marques in *Latter Rain Evangel*.

APPENDIX C

Appendix C
Faith Home Reports 1913-1915
[facsimiles of pages from Volume 1 Number 1
of FAITH journal,
compiled by
the Revs. Reuben A. and
Christine A. Gibson]

(Copy of) CHARTER
STATE OF RHODE ISLAND, ETC.

I, Charles P. Bennett, Secretary of State, hereby certify that Alpheus A. Cleveland, John Pennington, Andrew Munroe, Joseph T. Miller, John Norberry, F. M. Messenger, Jason T. Guild, Charles T. Potter, George W. Kies, Thomas C. Crocker have filed in the office of the Secretary of State, according to law, their agreement to form a Corporation under the name of Faith Home, East Providence, R. I., for the purpose of establishing a Home for homeless, evangelical Christian people in accordance with law, and have also filed the certificate of the General Treasurer that they have paid into the General Treasury of the State the fee required by law.

Witness my hand and the Seal of the State of Rhode Island, this 14th day of February, in the year 1901.

CHARLES P. BENNETT,
Secretary of State.

CONSTITUTION
of the
FAITH HOME OF EAST PROVIDENCE, R. I.

ARTICLE I. NAME

This Corporation shall be known as the Faith Home of East Providence, R. I.

ARTICLE II. OBJECT

Its object shall be to provide a Home for Homeless Evangelical Christian people, not otherwise provided for.

ARTICLE III. MEMBERSHIP.

The following incorporators, namely, A. A. Cleveland, John Pennington, Andrew J. Munroe, Joseph T. Miller, John Norberry, F. M. Messenger, Jason F. Guild, Charles T. Potter, George W. Kies and Thomas C. Crocker, with such additions as are provided for in Article V of the By-Laws, shall constitute the membership of this Corporation.

ARTICLE IV. OFFICERS.

There shall be chosen annually by ballot, a President, two Vice-Presidents, a Treasurer, a Clerk, a General Manager and an Auditing Committee of two.

ARTICLE V. DONATIONS AND BEQUESTS.

All sums of money received as donations, bequests, collections, or subscriptions, may be applied to the current expenses or to increase the Permanent Fund of the Corporation at the discretion of the Board of Directors unless otherwise specified by the givers.

ARTICLE VI. AMENDMENTS.

Alterations or amendments may be made to this Constitution at any meeting of the Corporation by a two-thirds vote of all the members present, provided that three months' notice in writing has been given to all the members stating the full text of the proposed change.

BY-LAWS.
ARTICLE I. OFFICERS.

The President shall preside at all meetings not otherwise provided for and shall call special meetings at the written request of five members, giving ten days' notice, specifying the object of the meeting. In absence of the President one of the Vice-Presidents shall preside, and in the absence of all of these, any member of the Corporation duly chosen shall preside.

ARTICLE II. TREASURER.

The Treasurer shall have the custody of all money, deeds, bonds, and securities belonging to the Corporation and draw the same on his order as Treasurer.

At the annual meeting he shall render a financial statement of the condition of the Corporation.

ARTICLE III. CLERK.

The Clerk shall notify members of all meetings of the Corporation, shall keep a record of all transactions, record names of all members present, shall notify the members of their election to office or appointment on committees and shall keep a record of all monies received.

ARTICLE IV. GENERAL MANAGER.

The General Manager shall have full charge of the Home and of the general business and property of the Corporation, subject to the Board of Directors.

ARTICLE V. VACANCIES.

Vacancies may be filled or additions made to the Corporation by a unanimous vote of the members present at any regular meeting, notice of such action having been given at the previous meeting.

ARTICLE VI. CANDIDATES FOR ADMISSION.

Homeless, evangelical Christians are eligible to admission to the Home.

ARTICLE VII. RULES.

All persons entering the Home are subject to its rules and to the direction of the General Manager. They shall attend family worship and other religious services in the Home unless physically unable.

ARTICLE VIII. AUDITORS.

The Auditors shall meet before the annual meeting and examine the Treasurer's books, and audit the same.

ARTICLE IX. MEETINGS.

Meetings of the Corporation shall be held the last Wednesday in March, June, September and the second Wednesday in December.

Five members shall constitute a quorum to do business, but a smaller number may adjourn.

ARTICLE X. ANNUAL MEETING.

Annual meeting of the Corporation shall be held on the second Wednesday of December of each year at Faith Home, East Providence, R. I., at which meeting the officers shall be elected, and such other business transacted as may be deemed necessary.

OFFICERS OF THE FAITH HOME OF EAST PROVIDENCE, R. I.
(Elected December 8, 1914.)

PRESIDENT,
Mrs. Antoinette B. Crocker .... 846 Broadway

VICE-PRESIDENTS,
Mrs. Ruth Cleveland .... 904 Broadway
Miss Emma K. Knowlton .... 846 Broadway

TREASURER,
Reuben A. Gibson .... 846 Broadway

CLERK,
Mrs. George W. Carpenter .... 5 Grosvenor Ave.

GENERAL MANAGER,
Reuben A. Gibson .... 846 Broadway

AUDITORS,
Albert Webb .... Montwait, Framingham, Mass.
Mrs. George W. Carpenter .... 5 Grosvenor Ave.

MATRON,
Mrs. Reuben A. Gibson .... 846 Broadway

RECEIPTS AND EXPENSES OF FAITH HOME
From June 1, 1913 to May 31, 1915.

Receipts

Donations	$2,827 68
Freewill offerings at parlor meetings and in freewill offering box	1,117 47
Sale of junk	4 25
Sale of Philo poultry houses	6 00
Sale of eggs	6 30
	$3,961 70

Expenses

General expenses	$2,150 29
Fuel	368 05
Lighting	143 33
House furnishings	228 49
Water tax	52 43
Repairs on buildings	204 56
Telephone	101 34
Interest on mortgage	360 00
Miscellaneous	101 56
Painting and paper hanging	58 56
Ice	39 57
Postage	8 37
Sewage assessment	109 35
Christian and Missionary Alliance	3 75
Printing letterheads and gospel tracts	34 68
	3,959 33
Balance on hand June 1, 1915	2 37
	$3,961 70

APPENDIX D

Appendix D
Chronology
of Zion Ministries*

(1) FAITH CHURCH
(Formally organized June 19, 1900 as
The Church of the First Born)

January, 1877-June, 1900...Rev. Alpheus Angel Cleveland, Founder/Pastor.

June, 1900 ....The name was changed from Faith Church to The Church of the First Born.

June, 1900-1908.....Rev. Alpheus Angel Cleveland, Pastor.

1908-February, 1948.......Rev. Christine A. Gibson, Pastor

February, 1948 ...The name was changed from The Church of the First Born to Zion Gospel Tabernacle

February, 1948-
November, 1954...........Rev. Christine A. Gibson, Pastor.

November, 1954..................The name was changed from Zion Gospel Tabernacle to Zion Gospel Temple.

November, 1954-
May, 1955 ....Rev. Christine A. Gibson, Pastor.

May, 1955-1960 ..Rev. Leonard W. Heroo, Interim Pastor.

1960-November, 1983 .....Rev. Leonard W. Heroo. Pastor.

November, 1983-
November, 1985 ....Rev. William K. Wilson, Pastor.

November, 1985-
September, 1991 ....Rev. Dr. Benjamin Crandall, Pastor.
September, 1991-present.....Rev. Douglas Crandall, Pastor.

*Courtesy of William "Bill" White of East Providence, Zion's "in-house" historian.

(2) FAITH HOME
(Established on February 24, 1877)
(Incorporated with first meeting held February 27, 1901)

February 24, 1877-1904 .... Rev. Alpheus Cleveland, Founder/Manager.
(Rev. Cleveland died August 10, 1908.)

1904-May 31, 1913 ....Rev. Thomas Crocker, Manager.
(Rev. Crocker died June 1, 1913.)

June 1, 1913-
May 5, 1924...............Rev. and Mrs. Reuben A. Gibson, Managers.
(Rev. Reuben A. Gibson died May 5, 1924.)

May 5, 1924-
May 31, 1955..........Rev. Christine A. Gibson, Manager.
(Rev. Christine A. Gibson died May 31, 1955.)

June 1, 1955-c. 1958 ....Managed by a Zion Administrative Committee.

In the late 50s, Faith Home, as such, ceased operations.

(3) CHILDREN'S HOME
c. 1918-1927 ....Alice Dunn Rich, Manager.
(located in Faith Home building, 846 Broadway, E. Providence)
1927-1938..........................Alice Dunn Rich, Manager.
(located at 46 Leonard Avenue, E. Providence).

1945-1956 .... Henry and Ethel Sinclair, Managers. (located at 838 Broadway, E. Providence).

(4) MOUNT ZION BIBLE SCHOOL

November, 1924-
May, 1925 .... Rev. Christine A. Gibson, Founder, President, and Principal.

September, 1925 .... The name was changed from Mount Zion Bible School to The School of the Prophets.

September, 1925-
May, 1935 .... Rev. Christine A. Gibson, President and Principal.

Diplomas were awarded for the school year of 1935/6 in the name of Zion Bible Institute. It has been called "Zion" from that time. However, the name was not legally changed until April 16, 1941.

September, 1935-
May, 1955 .... Rev. Christine A. Gibson, President and Principal.

June, 1955-1960 .... The presidency and principalship positions were handled by a Zion Administrative Committee.

1960-1983 .... Rev. Dr. Leonard W. Heroo, President.

1957-1981 .... Rev. Mary Campbell, Principal/Dean of Education.

1983-1985 .... Rev. Mary Campbell Wilson, President.

1981-1991 .... Rev. Eleanor Brunetto, Dean of Education.

1985-present .... Rev. Dr. Benjamin Crandall, President.

1991-present ..... Rev. Patrick Gallagher, Dean of Education and 2nd Vice President.

PHOTOGRAPHS

Rev. Alpheus Angel Cleveland
Founder of
Faith Home and Faith Church

●

Mrs. Adelaide Marian Cleveland

Rev. Christine A. Gibson
at the pulpit
Zion Gospel Tabernacle
●
c.1927

Rev. Reuben A. Gibson

Alice Rich (left) and
Christine Gibson

c.1920

Cottage-Eden Rest
Old Orchard, Maine

Rev. Christine A. Gibson (left)
and **Kathleen (Foster) Fischer**
(later, Mrs. Lester Goodwin)
●
c. 1927

Rev. Christine A. Gibson

•

c.1935

Rev. Christine A. Gibson
•
late 1930s

Rev. Christine A. Gibson
standing in front of Faith Home

•

c.1927

Faith Home
846 Broadway, East Providence, RI

•

c.1955

Soul Saving Station
Harlem, NY

•

Rev. and Mrs. Billy Roberts, Founders,
Rev. Christine Gibson, and Mary Campbell

Rev. N. Benjamin Crandall
standing on
Faith Home steps

Rev. Christine A. Gibson
•
Early 1950s

Rev. Dr. Leonard W. Heroo

Rev. and Mrs. E.B. Hill
"Buddy and Sylvia"

Alice Dunn Rich
•
c.1957

The Byron Hodgeman family

at their home in
East Providence, RI.

Back row, L to R
Melissa, Martin, Herbert, Russell, Jathneil, and Ramona.
•
Front row, L to R
Patty, Byron, Juddy, Marion, and David.

Alice Chase
•
1960s

Zion Gospel Temple
East Providence, Rhode Island

Zion Bible Institute
Barrington, Rhode Island

●

1992

"The joy of the whole earth."

About the Author

by
Patricia P. Pickard

Mary Ethel Campbell was born May 5, 1917, at Marsboro, Quebec, Canada, the daughter of Martin John and Annie Belle (MacKay) Campbell, residents of Boston, Massachusetts.

When Mary was quite young, her parents moved from Boston to Portland, Maine, where, in 1926, Mary was converted in a Pentecostal meeting. In 1933, she received the infilling of the Holy Ghost, with the evidence of speaking in tongues.

It was about this time that her mother began taking her to a little chapel in Old Orchard where Rev. Christine A. Gibson, president of Zion Bible Institute in East Providence, Rhode Island, preached during summer months.

Mary had a desire to take up the nursing profession; however, through a series of events, God closed the door to nursing, and opened the door of educational ministry in Mary's life.

In the fall of 1935, Mary enrolled at Zion Bible Institute, graduating in 1938. Sister Gibson became very fond of Mary and recognized her potential as an educator. Through this association, Mary became a teacher at Zion in the fall of 1939, teaching Bible Atlas. As the years rolled by, more subjects were added to Mary's teaching duties. These included, but were not limited to, Old Testament and Church History, the latter being her favorite subject to teach.

Around 1940/41, Mary was elected to serve on the board of directors of Zion Bible Institute, a position which she still holds. Summers were spent traveling with Sister Gibson, and spending time with her at Eden Rest, Zion's cottage at Old Orchard in Maine. Sister Gibson encouraged Mary to preach. At times, Mary felt she even resorted to *maneuvers* to get Mary behind a pulpit. In 1954, Mary supplied at the Exeter [Maine] Pentecostal Church for the summer, assisted by Charlene Hustus.

In 1957, after Sister Gibson's death in 1955, Mary became principal of Zion Bible Institute, holding that position until 1981. She received her bachelor's degree in Religious Education from Clarksville School of Theology in Tennessee. In 1969, she was "set apart" for the ministry, being ordained by the pastor of Zion Gospel Temple, Dr. Leonard W. Heroo. She still holds credentials with Zion.

During the summer months of the 1960s, Mary traveled extensively, visiting the Holy Land, European countries, the Caribbean Islands, including Barbados where Brother Gibson was born, and British Guiana in South America where Sister Gibson was born.

She has attended three Pentecostal World Conferences: Toronto, Ontario, Canada; Rio de Janeiro, Brazil; and London, England. In 1979, she visited former Zion students who were in ministry in Africa.

In later years she married Rev. William K. Wilson, a friend of many years. Their marriage took place in Zion Gospel Temple, East Providence, Rhode Island. The ceremony was performed by the Rev. Dr. Leonard W. Heroo, amidst a host of well-wishers and long-time friends.

Mary moved from the grounds of Zion where she had lived for nearly fifty years, to Rochester, New York, where "Bill" was pastoring a church. They remained there until 1983 when, once again, Zion called. Bill accepted the pastorship of Zion Gospel Temple and Mary became president of Zion Bible

Institute. They looked upon this as a temporary thing, because they knew that God had a man somewhere who was to fill both of these positions.

Rev. Dr. Benjamin Crandall was that man, and, as things were in good hands at Zion, Bill and Mary moved to Mars Hill, Maine, in 1987. Bill was ill and wanted to return to the place of his birth. Hence, Mary and Bill, along with Mary's aged mother, removed to northern Maine where Bill passed away in January of 1988.

The following year, Mary and her mother moved to Bangor, Maine, where Mary's mother passed away in a nursing home in January of 1992.

Mary spent the next three months in Florida working on this book, returning to Maine, where she worked on final details. As to Mary's future, she has this to say: *God's plan for my future will continue to unfold.*

Only one life — 'twill soon be past;
Only what's done for Christ will last.

(Selected)

Facsimile of greeting card given to Mary Campbell by Sister Christine Gibson.